THE

MOURNING

REPORT

THE

MOURNING

REPORT

CAITLIN GARVEY

Homebound Publications
Ensuring the mainstream isn't the only stream.

HOMEBOUND PUBLICATIONS
Ensuring the Mainstream Isn't the Only Stream | Since 2011
WWW.HOMEBOUNDPUBLICATIONS.COM

Quantity sales. Special discounts are available on quantity purchases by corporations, associations, bookstores and others. For details, contact the publisher or visit wholesalers such as Ingram or Baker & Taylor.

The author has tried to recreate events, locales and conversations from her memories of them. In order to maintain their anonymity, she has changed the names of individuals and places in some instances, and she may have changed some identifying characteristics and details, such as physical properties, occupations, and places of residence.

All Rights Reserved
Published in 2020 by Homebound Publications
Cover & Interior Designed by Leslie M. Browning
Cover Photo by © Caitlin Garvey
ISBN 978-1-947003-83-5
First Edition Trade Paperback

10 9 8 7 6 5 4 3 2 1

Homebound Publications is committed to ecological stewardship.
We greatly value the natural environment and invest in environmental
conservation. For each book purchased in our online store we plant one tree.
Visit us at: www.homeboundpublications.com

In memory of Denise Hogan Garvey

WE THROW OUR PARTIES; *we abandon our families to live alone in Canada; we struggle to write books that do not change the world, despite our gifts and our unstinting efforts, our most extravagant hopes. We live our lives, do whatever we do, and then we sleep. It's as simple and ordinary as that. A few jump out windows, or drown themselves, or take pills; more die by accident; and most of us are slowly devoured by some disease, or, if we're very fortunate, by time itself. There's just this for consolation: an hour here or there when our lives seem, against all odds and expectations, to burst open and give us everything we've ever imagined, though everyone but children (and perhaps even they) know these hours will inevitably be followed by others, far darker and more difficult. Still, we cherish the city, the morning; we hope, more than anything, for more.*

–MICHAEL CUNNINGHAM, *The Hours*

CHAPTER ONE

The Seed Collector

We learned "Head, Shoulders, Knees, and Toes" when I was in pre-school, and one kid tried to do the motions so fast that he made himself dizzy and threw up.

"Head, Shoulders, Knees, and Toes" is a children's song designed to get kids to learn their body parts and build motor skills—kids touch the sung body part. Every time it's sung, it gets a little bit faster. Other kids laugh if you can't keep up— if you get ahead of yourself and touch your knees instead of shoulders, or if you're winded from the motions and pause too long before touching your head. I had the most trouble with the "eyes and ears, and mouth and nose" part, so one day after school, I asked Momma if I could practice on her, touching her mouth before her nose. But we couldn't practice just that line—I had to sing every verse, starting with her head.

She laughed as we sat on the couch and I traced my hand along her features, and together we messed up the song on purpose, grabbing each other's noses or poking the other's ear. Eventually, though, we followed the order of the song, and as we synchronized our motions and bent down to touch our toes, I felt connected to her in a way that made me feel strong and soothed. I watched her as we started the song again from the top—she was tall and slim, with short blonde hair and soft blue eyes. In her body, she seemed powerful and free, and I remember wishing that I would grow overnight to look like her.

In 1997, when I was in second grade, Momma was diagnosed with chronic lymphocytic leukemia. On a day when I saw her vomiting from chemotherapy, I began to understand the limitations of the body. A cold could kill her, so my dad, two sisters, and I showed our love through air hugs and obsessive applications of hand sanitizer. We tried our best to kill germs, but at times we'd break the rules. A kiss goodnight on the cheek, a hug after a good grade, an uncovered sneeze, an accidental passing of the TV remote without first wiping it down. Germs infiltrated silently, leading to swollen hands, an infection, a private hospital room. I wished to trade bodies with her so that I could swallow her sickness, and she could be healthy and take care of me.

In 2001, after a few rounds of chemotherapy, Momma entered partial remission. But in 2005, when I was 15 and a sophomore in high school, she was diagnosed with stage IV inflammatory breast cancer, the most advanced stage and the deadliest kind of breast cancer. The cancer was too aggressive to not treat, even though doing so would further weaken her fragile immune system.

Momma was missing parts—her breasts, her hair, the good kind of white blood cells. In 2006, I watched her in the bathroom after her double mastectomy, even though she didn't want any family members to see her body. The plastic surgeon had removed lymph nodes from under her arm, but due to a complication of the surgery, her arm was severely swollen and more reminiscent of tree bark than human flesh. How painful it was to be graceful. Small things, like putting on blush, presented a big challenge. I stood behind the bathroom door, ready to come in if she needed me to help lift up her shirt or lean her weight on my arm so that she could take a shower. Through the crack in the door, I watched her shrinking. Her hair had fallen out and her shoulders had thinned. At 5'9", she was down to 100 pounds.

After her surgery, she was instructed to do daily physical therapy in the form of stretching her arm above her head. She put off the pain that the therapy involved, so I gave her a deadline. I drew horizontal black lines with a Sharpie on our bathroom wall. "You're at this line now," I pointed to the lowest one, before reaching to the highest one and saying, "Get here by November 1st."

"I have a better idea," she turned to me, smiling, and then wrote "24.9 seconds" on the highest line. "If I can get to that line by your November 1ˢᵗ swim meet, then you have to qualify for state with that time in the 50 freestyle." I laughed and then shook her hand to signify the closing of the deal. She did that a lot: diverted my attention away from her and forced me to focus on my high school life. As she stretched, I swam. I counted the seconds of my sprint to distract myself from guessing the number of days, or hours, that she had left. We both grew irritable from training. I could hear her grunt in pain in the bathroom as she tried to do her exercises. I came home from swim practice and collapsed on the couch. The more she stretched, the more I swam, the more I focused on the parts of my life that didn't concern her. The more she stretched, the more she wanted it that way.

On November 1ˢᵗ, 2006, I swam the 50 freestyle in 25.1 seconds, an arm's length away from the state-qualifying time. Momma, on the other hand, had stretched her fingers all the way to the top line in the bathroom, reaching her goal right before the swim meet. The day after the meet, the doctor told her that the cancer was spreading rapidly across the skin on her chest.

Her disease was a kind of slow violence. In the spring of 2008, after Momma had contracted multiple infections, the oncologist determined that any additional rounds of chemo would do more harm than good, so Momma went into hospice care. It wasn't until I watched her sleeping on a hospital bed in her own bedroom, surrounded by an oxygen tank, medicated gauze, and a catheter, that I was able to fully understand that some types of growth were actually types of decay.

I tried to speak to her on the night before she died. She was in her hospice bed and high on morphine. It was just the two of us in the room, and I stared at her as I sat in the chair next to her bed. Her mouth was open, and she was making sounds but not words, like she was trying to tell me something but couldn't get it out. I traced her mouth with my index finger. When I opened my own mouth to speak, I found myself mimicking her instead, making sounds but saying nothing.

I remember death's smell: the alcohol swabs we used to wipe her wounds, a greasy pillowcase mixed with the metallic smell of blood, Purell hand sanitizer, the smell of caramel Werther's mixed with urine from the catheter bag. I was 18 and home for summer break after my freshman year of college on June 8, 2008, the day Momma died. She looked small in her casket. Any trace of her fight with cancer was erased in the embalming. At her wake, when I thought no one was looking, I wiped off some of her blush. It was the last time I touched her.

Two years later, when I was in the second semester of my junior year at the University of Notre Dame, I tested the limits of my body. I took 30 Ambien pills, 10 mg each. After finding me in bed next to an empty pill bottle, my roommate drove me to the hospital, where a doctor studied me for a second and then asked, "Why did you take so many pills?" I answered, "I guess I wanted to kill myself." He said, with judgment, "You guess?" After a long, dizzying sensation and overnight hospital stay, I was admitted to a psychiatric center in South Bend, Indiana, a few blocks from campus. There, a therapist diagnosed me with "major depressive disorder and agitated anxiety," and I spent three weeks and four days as an inpatient.

It's been almost eight years since then. I have a career as an English lecturer, a stable relationship, a comfortable apartment in Chicago near my supportive family—to others, I may appear "healthy" or maybe even "happy." But most days, I feel the same heaviness that I felt on the night before she died, the burden that comes with feeling like everything is insignificant. Since 2010, I've tried 13 different medications, a mix of anti-depressants, anti-psychotics, anti-anxieties, and ADHD medications. I've had five different therapists. Still, I feel trapped in my body and trapped by a brain that constant-ly tells me I'm not good enough, or significant enough. I feel dead, but I can still hear my heartbeat.

My depression is binding—I feel stuck, like "Head, Shoulders, Knees, and Toes" is playing on repeat, but I can't keep up, and I feel confused and distant from myself, like I'm watching myself from the outside but can't control my ac-tions. My body is tired, and I feel much older than I actually am. Some days, when I'm stuck at a traffic light on my way to work, I stare at the people in the cars next to me, and I wonder how it feels to be them, and I wonder how freeing it must feel to be able to drive to work without considering crashing the car.

I'm scared to live, and I envy those who aren't scared.

Sometimes, I look at pictures of Momma and try to imagine the texture of her hair or the softness of her skin. But I don't remember what she feels like. She wore Ralph Lauren's "Blue" perfume, but when I spray it on my own wrists, it's unfamiliar. The scent lingers in the air, and I feel empty. I grieve for her, and I grieve for the mother I didn't get to know. I grieve over the gaps. I grieve for order, and I grieve for comfort.

*   *   *

The Buddhist parable of the mustard seed tells the story of a young woman, Kisa Gotami, who begs the Buddha for help after the death of her child. The Buddha tells her that he can bring her child back to life if she can collect mustard seeds from a family who hasn't experienced loss or suffering. Clutching her son's dead body to her bosom, Kisa travels from house to house, but each family gives her the same answer: they've all been touched by death and suffering, so she can't accept their mustard seeds.

She returns empty-handed to the Buddha, who lectures her about the cycle of human life and the impermanence of all things. Comforted by the Buddha's words, Kisa lays down the body of her child in a forest, and eventually, she becomes the Buddha's disciple.

I envy Kisa for being able to find peace, since I still feel like a child carrying her mother's weight. Momma's body is heavy, and I'm bound by it. While holding Momma's body, I feel abandoned, and like the body of Kisa's child, left in the woods. I'm screaming out for something I lost years ago and can't collect.

I have a recurring dream—in it, I dig and dig and dig. Momma doesn't have enough air down there, underground, and if I could just open the casket, if only for a little while, she could breathe fresh air.

Does the awareness of everything's mortality diminish the burdens of grief? And if it does, does it happen immediately? Kisa's ending seemed so false to my experience. I wondered what this sort of "grief journey" might yield for me, or how much truth there is to the feelings that Kisa has after her epiphany. I wondered if, like Kisa, I could find some solace in the process of collecting. I began this book out of desperation to feel unbound, to feel a comfort that could allow me to move forward in my life. I wanted to revisit my memories of the few days before and after Momma died, the moments when I felt the smallest and the most detached from the world. I hoped that I could pick up the pieces of myself that I left behind. I hoped to feel whole, not fragmented, and that I could remember more of Momma and get a fuller version of her story.

My process of collecting took the form of interviews. I interviewed five people, all of whom were a part of Momma's dying process: Momma's hairstylist and close friend, our family priest, a nurse and administrator at Heartland Hospice Care, my parents' estate planner, and an embalmer/funeral director. I thought that if I could figure out how these five people functioned after being so close to death, I could better navigate my own life. I hoped they could give me some guidance.

I want to let go of Momma's body, and instead, clutch her stories to my chest.

On her last birthday, less than a month before she died, Momma wouldn't take "no" for an answer, so her brother, my uncle Michael, took her outside. He removed her oxygen tube and lifted her into the wheelchair. He pushed her wheelchair down the back stairs to the yard, and her body bounced up from the seat as they went down one stair at a time. She didn't complain, and she smiled when she got outside. The sun was up, and despite the pain, she stretched her arms to the side. That was the last time she went outside.

I want the promise of progress, and I want to feel warm, and alive, even if my heart is failing.

In Sunday school, we learned that a mustard seed is a symbol for the Kingdom of Heaven—it's smaller than all other seeds, but when grown, it "becomes greater than all the herbs, and puts out great branches, so that the birds of the sky can lodge under its shadow" (Mark 4:30-32). I wish I could feel that powerful. I want the good kind of growth. I dream of a bigger life, and I dream of a return to a sense of wonder.

CHAPTER TWO

The Hairstylist

A Lana Del Rey song comes on the radio as I'm driving from my Chicago neighborhood to Oak Park, the suburb where I grew up. Del Rey's voice is low and strange as she sings, "Dancing in the dark in the pale moonlight," and I turn up the volume to drown out the loud rumbling of the car next to me. The drive usually takes about half an hour, but I'm stuck on Lake Shore Drive in afternoon rush-hour traffic that hasn't moved for over 10 minutes. I gave myself plenty of time to get to Oak Park for my interview, but I still feel anxious. It's hard for me to breathe whenever I feel closed in, and when I look at the line of cars in front of me and behind, my hands start shaking and my mouth dries up. I didn't bring any Klonopin with me, so I calm myself by inhaling and exhaling slowly, and I try to focus on the lyrics. I try to trick myself into thinking that I'm somewhere else, or someone else, like Lana.

I run my hands through my hair and imagine that it's longer and smoother, like hers, and I'm in the moonlight, dancing alone, alive and fearless and free.

After over an hour and a half of driving, I pull into the Starbucks parking lot in Oak Park, where I'm meeting hairstylist Debbie Musso. Away from the traffic jam, I feel calmer, but when I think about what it will be like to see Debbie after almost 10 years, my heart rate speeds up again. I'm 15 minutes early, so I stay in my car and look out my window at a mother and daughter, who are linking arms and smiling as they walk into the beauty store next to Starbucks. The girl is maybe 15, and she's wearing a sweatshirt with a husky mascot on it that says "Oak Park-River Forest," the name of my former high school. Her mom has short blonde hair that reminds me of Momma's, and as I watch the two of them go into the store, I feel sad.

I'm still a few minutes early, but I head into the Starbucks anyway. I feel more comfortable when I can have some control over a social setting, like being able to choose the table. I'm not a big coffee drinker, and the Starbucks menu overwhelms me with options, so I just order the same thing as the woman in line in front of me—a tall caramel macchiato. Still wanting to escape my anxiety and myself, I tell the barista my name is "Lana" and pay in cash, and then I pick a quiet seat near the window.

Debbie was one of Momma's closest friends. My two sisters and I are around the same age as her two kids, and the five of us went to St. Giles, a Catholic school in Oak Park, from pre-school through eighth grade. The St. Giles community is small—almost all of the families know each other, or at least recognize each other from Sunday mass—so Debbie and Momma connected through their involvement in school events and fundraisers. When my sisters and I were at St. Giles, Debbie ran a hair salon out of her basement, so we became even closer to her family as we started going to her house for haircuts. She cut my hair in her basement starting when I was in kindergarten and continuing until my senior prom. I stopped seeing her when Momma died—it was harder for me to find time during my breaks from college, and I don't get my hair cut very often anyway.

Before I had Klonopin to "shield me" from social anxiety, I had Momma, who introduced me to her friends. I clung to the back of her shirt and every few seconds peered my head out from her side to see if they were gone yet. "Hi, Caitlin!" they would sweetly say, trying to cajole me from the comforts of Momma's clothes. "She's just shy," Momma would say. "Don't take it personally."

Debbie and Momma frequently got together with a few other St. Giles moms—sometimes the six or seven women would drink wine in the living room of my house, and I'd listen in on their conversations as I sat on the staircase, hidden behind the wall. They talked about books, politics, other moms, and work, and they laughed about their kids' behaviors. They seemed happy and smart and free. They had an intimacy and a closeness that I envied. The women were privy to information about her life and health that I never knew. Momma had decided that my sisters and I were too young to know everything about her cancer and its progression, so she kept a lot of the realities of her illness hidden from us, like what stage IV really meant, and how dangerous it really was if her white blood cell counts weren't high enough for her to receive chemotherapy treatment. She frequently dismissed its seriousness by telling my sisters and me things like, "Doctors just say stuff with Latin words to sound smart." Debbie, though, knew more of the real story and understood the stakes, and she was always ready to help Momma in any way that she could—this included shaving Momma's head before it fell out from chemo, taking Momma wig shopping, and after treatment stopped and Momma was in hospice, shampooing Momma's hair.

There was so much I wanted to say and ask Momma but never felt I could; maybe the number of questions was overwhelming, a too-short glimpse into the intricacies of her life before it got taken away, or maybe, most likely, I just didn't know how to deal with the idea of her death. I wanted to know what she was like as a kid, as a teenager; I wanted to know if she ever did anything rebellious; I wanted to know if she was scared; I wanted to know if she regretted her career in law; I wanted to know if she regretted giving up law at age 35 to become a mother; I wanted to know if there was hope; I wanted to know what I should do if there was no hope. She was a stranger to me in many ways. When she died, I found her old journals. I read them every day, trying to make the image of her more complete. But as I read them, I felt weird—they weren't meant for me to see, and I was violating her privacy. And even after I read them, she still felt unfamiliar to me, and I had more questions about her life than when I started.

Even though I understood that she was dying, I never felt prepared for it. Maybe Debbie had more of Momma's story. Even though I recognize there's a difference between losing a mother and losing a friend, I wondered if Debbie felt more prepared for Momma's death or at least coped in ways that could potentially help me, too, and I wanted to interview her to find out.

After Momma died, my younger sister, Sarah, then 15 years old, started collecting moms. She visited Momma's friends and other moms in the Oak Park community, and she talked to them frequently and kept them updated on her life. She asked them for help when she needed it, and they gave it. From them, she got some instruction and guidance, but also warmth and closeness. I was always too shy, or scared, to reach out to anyone in that way. I kept my emotions to myself and hid the parts of myself, like depression and anxiety, that I didn't want other people to see. Maybe, by talking to Debbie, even if only for a few hours, I could not only feel closer to Momma, but also to Debbie. Maybe I could feel the calm that comes from confiding in someone, the peace that Kisa feels in the parable when she speaks to families about her suffering and theirs.

*   *   *

Debbie walks into Starbucks with a springy step—she says "hi" to me before ordering. A few minutes later, drink in hand, she hugs me and takes the seat across from me. "You look like your mother," she says while smiling. "You have her eyes." I smile back and feel happy and warm, but I worry that I will disappoint her—there's a sadness to her voice that makes me wish I were Momma instead of myself so that I could give Debbie back the friend she lost.

I used to worry that I would disappoint Debbie, too, when I was younger and her client. I was a shy and anxious kid, and uncomfortable in my body—I had difficulty making conversation with anyone, especially parents, and I worried that I bored her because I stayed silent as she styled my hair. When I was in grammar school and staring at the mirror in Debbie's basement, I remember wishing I were invisible. Haircuts, to this day, make me feel incredibly awkward. I never have the language for what cut I want, so I always say, "Just a trim." My neck hurts from holding my head back in the sink, but I say "not at all" when a stylist asks if I'm uncomfortable. And in the chair, I never know where to look—do you look in the mirror and stare at yourself as the stylist is blow-drying, or if that's vain, do you look at your hands? I usually do more looking down, but I peek a lot in the mirror. Still, I pretend every time, when the stylist says he's done, that my haircut is such an incredible surprise and I can't wait to go out to the club later to show everyone. I don't go to clubs, but this is my default answer for when the stylist, desperate for me to say something of interest, asks if I have "any fun plans" for after my haircut. And, after I leave the salon, I always pull my hair back into a ponytail once I'm in my car.

After Momma died, I changed my appearance a lot. I chopped my hair off; I gained weight; I lost a lot of weight; I obsessed about my body and stared at mirrors. Each time I stared at the mirror, though, I felt the same as I did when I was a kid—I hoped that nothing would be reflected back. I remember, as a 13-year-old, staring at my reflection with a mix of fear, confusion, and awe. I had just gotten a haircut from Debbie, and I thought it made my face look even chubbier than usual. My whole body felt large and cumbersome. Momma came in the room and saw me trying to part my hair at a different angle. She walked behind me, arched my shoulders back, and whispered as we faced the mirror, "You are so beautiful." I watched her face in the mirror instead of looking at myself—there was nothing awkward about her hair or her features; her skin was smooth, and her body looked strong. She was healthy. Her blonde hair was coiffed, every strand in place. Momma's touch on my shoulder was gentle, and it made me feel calm. When she eventually walked toward the door, I wanted to tell her to come back, to stay in the room with me for a little while longer. I wanted to ask her if I was normal, if I was going to be okay, and I wanted to prolong puberty, to have her linger there in that moment before I had to navigate my new body and adulthood alone.

Debbie is 60 years old, but she looks much younger, the same way I remember her. Her hair is curly—brown but with a reddish tint—and she wears bright red lipstick and a sleeveless red dress that shows off her biceps. She's stylish and seems sure of herself, and she speaks loudly and clearly. I wish I could be as confident as she seems, and I hope that if I make it to 60, I'll be just as vibrant. As she faces me, I wonder if she's looking at my hair and able to see all my split ends, or judging me for using a box dye, and I wish that, instead of waiting in my car, I had gone into the beauty store and bought some lipstick.

As we sip our coffee (and I learn that I don't like caramel macchiatos), I ask Debbie how she got her start as a hairstylist. She talks, first, about her childhood and her family dynamic. She grew up in Elmhurst—she has an older brother, but she's the oldest of four girls, and she describes her parents as "typical, 100 percent Italian, with strict rules, like making their kids live in the house until they got married." Her parents taught her the importance of generosity. She tells me that she "paved the way" for her siblings—her dad had a chronic bone disease, so as a teenager, Debbie took on the responsibility of caring for her siblings, doing things like cooking, cleaning, and helping them with homework. She says that she was shy and antisocial throughout grade school and high school because she was dealing with the demands of her home life. As a teenager, she didn't get to go out much, and she didn't have many friends, but she doesn't resent that—she was always going to put her family first.

Debbie says her parents weren't wealthy, but they put all of their kids through college. She fell in love with hair when she was a student at Eastern Illinois University—she spent her free time doing her sorority sisters' hair, as well as her boyfriend's—and through hair, she became more outgoing, expressing herself through the art form and forging friendships with the students whose hair she styled. Her major was in clothing design, so she used the scissors she had from those classes to cut their hair. She laughs and says, "Now, this was the '70s, so accuracy wasn't a requirement." Still, she felt happiest when she was doing hair, and she wanted to get better at it. She knew, though, that her parents wouldn't be happy if she told them she wanted to go to beauty school. Her dad, especially, wanted her to graduate from college because he hadn't gone himself, and he had hoped for something better for her. So, to appease him, she graduated and worked for a year as a store manager. Eventually, though, she felt unfulfilled by the work and decided to pursue beauty school. To afford it, she traded in the car that her parents had bought her on her college graduation.

"I was determined," she says, "so I waitressed at night and went to beauty school during the day. And I did that in nine months—1,500 hours, full-time and waitressing at night." Her dad wouldn't let Debbie cut his hair when she was in beauty school, but she tells me that within the first year, she "bought a car paid in all cash, and a fur coat"—and when he saw that, he was proud of her. After that, he asked her to cut his hair every two weeks. Debbie's worked as a hairstylist for 37 years now—in addition to cutting hair in her basement for 19 years, she's worked in four other salons. Her voice is frequently hoarse because of how much she talks to her clients.

Debbie is charismatic and chatty—she controls the flow of conversation, and there's something about how she talks with her hands that puts me at ease. She loves the intimacy of haircutting, she says. She says she's a perfectionist and often texts her clients after their visits to make sure they're satisfied. And she's not just a hairdresser, she says, but more of a "part-time therapist, like a bartender." She gives her clients advice, and vice versa—they trade parenting tips, and career and relationship advice. Each one of her clients is her friend, she says, "because of the years, the longevity." When clients used to come to her basement, there'd be hair all over her house—her kids would find clumps of it on the kitchen table, and they'd just wipe it off and continue eating. "Cutting hair in your own home just brings you so much closer to your clients," she says.

She continues, "I remember when you guys came into my life—you guys were so young. I had the little TV down there in the basement, and we put cartoons on for you girls, and your mom would sometimes come over during the day to get her hair color done while you guys were at school." She remembers that Sarah—"that little redhead"—loved to sweep up the hair from the floor. "Most people are grossed out by the hair on the floor," she says, "but Sarah loved it." I picture my sister, maybe four years old, tidying hair into piles in the basement corner.

Debbie talks about hair's importance to beauty, the social stigma that bald women face, and the naked feeling that comes from baldness. She says that whenever she walks into a room, hair is the first thing she sees. "Your hair adorns you," she says, adding, "Even if bald women wear a cap or a fedora, people can still see that there's no hairline, and that's a big vulnerability. Plus, hair keeps you warm." It's about control, she says. "You get to choose its color, texture, and length. Then somebody, or something—illness—takes that away from you, and you lose choice, and you lose the control you had."

"Your hair speaks for you," Debbie says. "And I think that people try out more hairstyles when they're young. I think when you're older you find other parts of your life that mean more than your hair. There's less rebellion."

When she says this, I remember the time when my older sister, Meaghan, then 14 years old, came home with blue hair. "That's a bright color on you," Momma delivered matter-of-factly, with a straight face. A wannabe rebel driven by the prospect of pissing parents off, Meaghan was understandably devastated by this reaction. She stomped all the way upstairs, and behind her slammed door we could hear sobbed renditions of, "Oh, my God, no one understands me!" and "They're ruining my life!" and finally, a little quieter, after a brief pause and less frequent sniffles, "Fuck. It looks terrible."

A few days later, Momma observed the weather. "It's raining hard," she said at the breakfast table. "And I suppose that's my fault?" came Meaghan's indignant retort, to which Momma burst out laughing. Each minute of her heavy bellow loosened Meaghan's glare, so when I joined in and, seconds later, so did my little sister, our united cacophony gave Meaghan hardly any choice but to give in, too. Then the laughter quieted down a bit, and as we caught our breaths and wiped a couple tears from our eyes, Meaghan squeaked, "Wait, what are we going to do about my hair?" which had us laughing all over again.

A few years after that, it was my senior prom. I've always hated getting dressed up, but I especially hated the process for my prom. An hour before the dance, I was trying to undo the hairstyle that Debbie had given me because it felt too fancy—it was curly updo, and I'd hoped for something that looked "effortless"—but I made a mess of it. "Momma!" came my piercing scream from the upstairs bedroom. "Get these bobby pins off of my head!" Momma started, "For the love of God, Caitlin, if you hadn't fussed with it in the first place…" and I fired back, "How do you even know what looks good? You don't even have hair." Then came, "Fine. Fix it yourself," and after a slammed door and a few more exchanged of "Fine!" and "I hate you!" she heard a soft, defeated, "Okay, I'm sorry," which preceded an even more delicate, "Please help." When I finally finished fussing with it, she narrowed her eyebrows and muttered, "You looked better before."

I took out my anger on my hair when Momma had none. Momma was dying, and her body was destroying itself from the inside out—and I didn't want to live in a body that was healthy, or with a head full of hair, if she couldn't have that, too. If her body was collapsing, I wanted to destroy mine—I didn't deserve to be able to wear a fancy prom dress or have a hairstyle that would look good in pictures. I felt angry all the time, and I needed to escape my situation in any way I could, trying out different hairstyles or new identities.

When I was 16, Momma had a double mastectomy, and I had my first beer. A senior girl on my swim team, whom I had to impress, lived adjacent to a forest preserve, and after she watched me take a few sips from the beer she handed me, she nodded, seemingly content that I passed her test, and whispered, "Come on, we're meeting people," and I followed as she led me through her backyard. It was a chilly October night, and walking behind her, I stumbled over tree branches and leaves that I couldn't see in the dark. The woods were for the Cool Kids—the ones who ditched school assemblies to get high and blew the smoke into the security guards' faces, the ones who called their parents by their first names, the ones who worshipped Jack Kerouac. They threw their empty beer cans behind the trees and didn't give a fuck about anything or anyone. They lived in pursuit of the party. They seemed free. I wanted to get lost with them.

My hand was cold from the beer but my head was hot. I was sitting by myself on a horizontal tree trunk that had fallen during a heavy storm, and around me a few strangers had started a campfire and set up a keg. The girl who brought me there had gone off to make out with one of the keg carriers, so I played a quiet drinking game with myself, which involved swallowing giant gulps of the cheap beer whenever I had to talk to someone. The beer smelled strongly of skunk spray when I put it up to my lips and I wanted to go home, but I would never tell anyone there. A sweaty boy with beer dribbling down his chin and onto his shirt approached me and extended his hand.

"Nate."

I took a swig.

"Caitlin."

"You look like you need a refill."

I looked down at my cup and found nothing but a mass of solid matter floating near the bottom. He looked, too.

"Ooh, you've got floaties. Could be a yeast chunk."

He took out a can of Natty Light beer from his shirt pocket and opened it, releasing a gush of foam that eagerly escaped down his fingers. He held the can away from him but toward me.

"Here, you better drink fast."

He laughed as I tried to slurp up the thin layer of liquid that pooled over the can tab on its flat top, and then he said I was a "pro at this," and that I was too quiet, and why didn't I look like I was having fun? His words faded in and out, but to satisfy him I slurred out a string of "yesses" and "I don't knows" between shy smiles and nervous nodding. "So my buddy got his older brother to buy booze in exchange for a hot girl's number ... we should do this every weekend ... there's a party at Matt's house next Thursday ... you should smile more ... do you need another beer?"

Then he put his arm around my shoulder, lingering for a few minutes before his fingers crept down my shoulder, spider-like, and reached under the neck of my shirt for my breast. With one finger he made a few small circles around my bra until my silence spoke to his other fingers to join, and in unison they felt up my chest. And soon, not just my head but my whole body felt hot, and the trees were spinning a little out of focus and his ceaseless squeezing made everything feel so stupid, and when would it stop? The heat was intensifying, and I wondered if someone could explode at this temperature, and I wondered if I wanted to. My toes were so hot until, suddenly, they were wet. I looked up to see one of the guys holding an empty bucket and laughing.

"Shit, girl, your shoe caught fire!"

I looked down at the melted plastic toe of my sneaker and the fire embers that had tumbled out of the flames.

I rode home in the passenger seat of a drunk girl's swerving car, and I called Momma.

*   *   *

Debbie's eyes widen as she talks about hair, and I think about the power of finding a passion for something and being successful doing it. In 1993, four years before Momma's leukemia diagnosis, Momma wrote the following journal entry:

I am 37 years old. I'm not sure who I am when I stand alone. I feel like David Copperfield: "If I be the hero of my own life or if this station shall be held by some-one else, these pages shall tell." I only wish that I could write as well as Charles.

I once could write, and I once enjoyed it. I should say that I once showed promise. I did win the NCTE achievement award in writing in high school, and I never received less than an "A" in an English class. But I've never been published, and I have not attempted to write more than a friendly letter since college. I think that I shunned the amount of effort and solitude a career in writing would require (or at least what I imagined it would require).

So here I sit in my kitchen (I hate the décor), trained as a lawyer and practicing domesticity. I'm ambivalent about my life's choices. I never enjoyed law, but I found it difficult to give up. I love Ed and the girls, but I often feel trapped within the confines of this 1920s Oak Park home.

But what occurs to me now is that the choices I've made were precisely what I wanted. I avoided writing, which would have required me to expose my weakness-es (as well as my strengths), and chose a field in which I would be less vulnerable. I hid behind expensive suits and legalese and enjoyed a profession in which I never had to reveal myself—I was always arguing for and negotiating on behalf of my client. I was merely a spokesperson; I wasn't speaking on my own behalf.

I wrap myself in the cloak of motherhood and defend the rights of my children while perhaps losing myself as well. This may be intentional; I'm not sure I wish to undrape myself, not even within the narrow confines of my home.

Momma hid, too, and she was still trying to figure herself out. She spoke on behalf of Meaghan, Sarah, and me, and then it wasn't long after that when her illness spoke on behalf of her. Inhabiting her body and destroying it from the inside out, her illness eventually became her identity. Cancer takes. It leaves loss in its place—a bald head, pale skin, a flat chest. I wonder how Momma felt when she looked in the mirror and watched parts of herself disappearing. Cancer robbed her of some control, and she was forced to expose some of the things she would have preferred to hide.

Debbie talks to me about her experience with wig shopping with Momma—they went to a place called Naturally Yours. Before she tried on different wigs, Momma turned to Debbie and said, "Let's just get this over with." They eventually bought one, but Momma never wore it. The wig was uncomfortable for Momma because her medication made her scalp sensitive, Debbie says, and she speculates, too, that Momma felt the wig was too artificial-looking. Still, it seems like Momma's choice to not wear the wig (but a black cap instead) speaks to some of the control that she tried to take over her cancer—she made decisions about whom she would tell, as well as how little information she could get away with telling my sisters and me. And she tried to escape the sounds of her illness. When the cancer spread farther across Momma's chest, it created a gaping chest wound that ultimately led to a skin graft—"fresh skin" replacing unhealthy tissue. She was prescribed a Wound V.A.C. (Vacuum-Assisted Closure) for the healing process. The V.A.C.—the size of a shoebox— made sucking noises as Momma held onto it, like a portable vacuum, reminding her of its constant presence. Attached to a tube that was sealed onto her wound with a sponge, the V.A.C. was supposed to draw the edges of her wound together and suck out infectious materials. On several days, Momma asked me to play my trumpet for her. "It's nice, just for a little bit, to mute the sound of the suction," she said, as she sat on our living room couch and listened.

When I was 18 and in my freshman year of college, I called Momma whenever I didn't know something or needed help. She said, "Remember to take your vitamins," and reminded me that I was irritable because I wasn't eating enough. She said, "Talk to the shy girls because they're usually the funni- est," and ordered me to go to Health Services when I had a blister on my toe. She said, "Turn off the sad music and go to class," and reminded me to swim when I wasn't feeling like myself. I hoped she would decide who I was—I couldn't be

sure of anything until I heard her voice. That year, I sometimes skipped classes and avoided hanging out with other
students, and instead I spent hours on the Internet, creating
fake Facebook profiles. I found pictures of random young
adults on Google, and I used their images as their profile
pictures. I invented names for my characters and befriended
people I didn't know. I invented personalities for the people
in my profiles—they lived in places like California and New
York, with jobs like travel photographer, personal trainer,
and flight attendant—and they were good-looking and confident, and it was easy for me to talk to people on Facebook
chat when I hid behind the false profiles. On nights when I
couldn't sleep, I desperately wished to wake up as one of the
people I'd invented.

As each year passes, I become less sure what kind of advice
Momma would give me, and even what her voice sounded
like. The silence is replaced by a voice that tells me I'm un-
worthy of life, and most days, I feel controlled by it. I'm mad
at myself for wanting to die when all Momma wanted to do
was live.

There are invisible aspects to every illness. This past year,
I started displaying symptoms of an impulse control disorder
called trichotillomania—for me, it's characterized by repeti-
tively pulling out my eyebrow hairs, and it's at its worst when
I feel stressed. Each eyebrow hair feels like a weight, and I
feel less burdened by them the more I pull, like I'm releasing

myself from something, and some days, I can't stop pulling until every hair is gone. I cover the loss of eyebrow hair with makeup. As I pick out each hair, I feel a similar sense of relief to when I overdosed on sleeping pills—each pill that I swallowed made me feel calmer and more in control, the possibility of a permanent escape. And before I swallowed the pills, I put on makeup and curled my hair—if I was going to die, at least people would see what I wanted them to.

*　　*　　*

When Momma was in hospice, her straight hair grew back curly. Debbie came to our house every week during this time, and she'd wash Momma's hair in the bathroom off of my parents' bedroom. Debbie says, "The sink was low enough so she could lean forward and I'd wash her hair like that. When she was in a wheelchair, we'd wash her hair and I'd blow dry it, and after, she'd always say, 'Oh, I feel so good.'" Debbie says that she felt "honored to do her hair and help her this way" because Momma "was such a private person."

I find out that Debbie styled Momma's hair for her wake. Although this task is usually reserved for the embalmer, Momma had requested that Debbie do it. When my dad called to ask if she would, Debbie didn't hesitate. "I'm there; just tell me when," she said. This was another intimate moment that Debbie got with Momma, so I ask her what she was feeling. Debbie looks down as she answers, and she speaks in a quieter voice, like she's reliving it. "I was talking to her, to be honest," she says. "Talking out loud, like we were having a normal visit."

At recess in fifth grade, I remember overhearing a classmate who, trying to scare his friend, said that hair and nails continue growing on a dead body. It was several years before I looked into the credibility of his claim—throughout those years, though, I imagined a corpse, discolored, zombie-like, buried under the earth, but strangled by hair so long it cracked the lid of the coffin and eventually broke through the grass to continue growing above ground. I didn't believe in spirits, just hair-flooded cemeteries.

Debbie says that Momma had her "real hair all back by then," and that it's easier to do natural hair than it is to do a wig. With a dead person, she says, "you just do the sides and the top, two-thirds of it, but you have to get it to lay and make it look full." She says she feels fortunate to have gotten that time with Momma. "What I've carried with me through these years," she says to me, "is what your father said when he came up to me when we were about six people away from your mom's casket. He said, 'I want you to know that the reason my daughters can stand there next to the casket and feel that their mom looks familiar is because you did her hair.'"

I feel so connected to Debbie as she talks about this—it seems that almost 10 years hasn't made it much easier for her, either. The memory is still so alive. I picture myself at Momma's wake, standing next to her casket. I was smiling and laughing with the people who attended, and I was speaking clearly as I shared memories of Momma with them and thanked them for coming. I was outgoing and relaxed, like someone had taken over my body to give me a break for the day.

Momma was the second person whose hair Debbie styled for a wake. Mostly as a favor to a co-worker whose father is an undertaker, Debbie has dressed hair for 12 dead people. The first time she did it, it was for her father. She was just 29 years old when he died. "My dad had hair that looked like Dean Martin, a pompadour," she says, "and when we went to view him in the casket, they had it all greased back like Dracula. So my mom looked at me and said, 'Debbie, can you fix this?'" Debbie approached the undertaker and demanded "a towel, a comb, baby powder, and hairspray." She continues:

> I draped him with the towel because he had his suit on. I put baby powder in his hair because it breaks down the gel, and I ruffled his hair and got all the baby powder out. He was the first dead body I'd ever touched, and when I ruffled his hair, I made him look exactly like himself. I kind of just felt like God gave me a talent, and if I'm the instrument that can make my family or another family feel more familiar with the dead body, then so be it.

I ask Debbie about the loss of her father, and grief, and if she's experienced it as a cycle, or in stages. She has pictures of her dad all over her house, she says, "and when I look at my son, he looks so much like my dad. I think you turn around and get to a point where you see your life as more of a gift, and you're able to move forward without them physically present." Even when dealing with grief, Debbie seems active and in control, "turn[ing] around" and "mov[ing] forward." She's able to do this, she says, by continuing to work and immerse herself in her clients' stories and experiences. "I have just under 300 clients," she says, "so that's a lot of stories to fill my life." She says, too, that she feels better when she's able to do things for people. "I always tell my kids this, and I want to say this came from your mom," she says, "but I tell them, 'Live your life how you want to be remembered, and if you want to be remembered as a giving, caring person,' as your mom was, 'then you know you've done well.'"

She seems like the type of person who just "does it"—she's strong-willed, a "strong Italian," as she calls herself, valuing action over introspection. When I ask Debbie how she pictures her future, she replies, "As long as my hands can keep doing what they do, I'll keep making people feel good."

When she says this, I think of the hour before Momma's wake when my sisters and I were donning dark dresses and diving deep into the distractions of getting ready. On the floor next to us lay discarded tights, curling irons, shoes, and hairspray, all the products of running late.

"Can I borrow your lipstick?" Sarah asked.

"Yes, if I can have your dark eyeliner."

"Don't wear those shoes; they're not wake-y enough."

"Shit, I don't have tights—do you think this dress will still look good?"

And, finally, "What are you gonna do with your hair?"

I couldn't help smiling when I asked Sarah how mine looked, and she innocently replied, "Better before you styled it."

*   *   *

Every summer starting when I was about six, up until I was 14 (our summers eventually got too busy), Momma had Meaghan and me write fictional stories based on a single line that she'd cut out from a newspaper. We had an hour to write, after which Momma judged our stories and determined which one was best—Meaghan had a two-year advantage and was a stronger writer, but sometimes Momma would let me win. As her journal indicates, a writer, to Momma, was a very public person, someone who maintained a level of confidence that she herself might have lacked, a person who wrote to be read and "exposed." I think Momma hoped that we could avoid feeling this way—with the writing contest she controlled, we could feel safe in our expression—competitive, but confident, and welcoming of this kind of vulnerability. Momma gave us constructive criticism while also celebrating our stories. This kind of invention made me feel free, and I loved having the power to construct a narrative.

At night, we'd celebrate the completion of our stories by listening to books and other stories that Momma would read us. Sometimes, I would sit between Momma's legs on my carpeted bedroom floor and close my eyes as she read stories, like "The Gift of the Magi," to us. I lost myself in the characters. O. Henry's character Della sells her beloved hair to pay for her husband's Christmas present, a gold watch chain. O. Henry writes, "Della's beautiful hair fell about her, shining like a falling stream of brown water. It reached below her knee. It almost made itself into a dress for her." Without her hair, Della is naked and exposed. Wrapping itself around her body, her hair consumes her. It's her identity. But selling her hair is in vain—her husband, Jim, has pawned his watch to buy her a comb.

As I sit across from Debbie, I think of the visibility of sacrifice in "The Gift of the Magi." Debbie helped my family in more ways than hair. Along with the "network of moms" from the St. Giles and Oak Park community, she made meals and delivered them to our house when Momma was sick. The meals were elaborate—along with a main course, there was usually an appetizer and there was always dessert.

Della chooses to sell part of what makes her "her" to demonstrate her love for Jim. O. Henry calls this unwise, the idea of selling the most valuable thing you own in order to buy a gift for someone else. But he also writes that, among all those who "give and receive gifts," Della and Jim are the wisest—they value each other's happiness over their own. They give despite the self-imposed burdens of giving.

In religion class at St. Giles, we learned that after Jesus was born, the magi traveled to Jerusalem and asked, "Where is the one who has been born king of Jews? We have seen His star in the East and have come to worship Him." They came to give gifts because they saw the star, their active journey prompted by this visibility. The magi brought gifts of gold, frankincense, and myrrh. Biblical scholars say the gold symbolized kingship and divinity. Frankincense, a white resin, symbolized holiness and his ultimate righteous sacrifice, and myrrh, a spice used in the embalming process, represented his suffering and death.

Debbie dressed Momma's hair, returning to her some of her identity, or at the very least, making Momma "feel so good," if only for a moment.

Before we say goodbye to each other at Starbucks, Debbie says, "Your mom is with us now. I feel that."

Spirituality is strange because it's invisible. You have to feel it. In that moment, I feel something, too. I feel warm, like I felt when Momma would comb out the knots in my hair and then blow-dry it before I went to school.

On my drive back to Chicago, I remember a candid photograph of Momma and her friends, all standing in a circle and laughing by Lake Michigan, and I roll down my car window, smile, and let myself feel the breeze.

CHAPTER THREE

The Priest

In 1998, when I was in fourth grade, Momma wrote a journal entry that discusses her impending chemotherapy treatment for the leukemia:

> Surprise. There is to be no treatment, at least not until after the holidays. I'm relieved, but a large part of me is angry. Last week was pure hell. I met with Maureen and Patrice [St. Giles friends] to "organize" in the event things went badly. I felt stripped bare. I felt as if my life and lifestyle were under critical scrutiny. It also made me fear for the girls. In the days that followed up to the doctor's appointment, I couldn't sleep much, and when I could, I had horrible nightmares about the children. I lost five pounds. I was terrified.

And now it's over. Momentarily. I feel I feel myself being sucked into depression. I'm annoyed by every-day events. I'm tired. I'm having difficulty adjusting to dealing with these days that I hadn't planned on deal-ing with. I'm confused. I feel fat and sluggish. I don't know what to do. I fear going forward and having to face the treatment option again …

I can't hide from this disease or the feelings I have about it. I can't try to be what others, or more apt-ly, what I think others want from me. I just have to be myself and accept it, with all its inadequacies and strengths. I need to repair. I can't repair the disease or my body, but I can repair my relationships, which are worn thin by the stress of this ordeal.

I've worked so many years on improving my mind. Now I need to work on the emotions that I have so skillfully hidden.

That year, my class was preparing to receive the Sacrament of Reconciliation, and we learned that there were different kinds of sins, big and small ones, mortal and venial. "Mortal sin is like a malignant tumor that critically hurts our spiritual life and our relationship with God," our religion teacher re-peated each week. Small sins included gossip and accidental swearing, and big sins included things like murder, sacrilege, divorce, and suicide. I was particularly scared of the "sin of omission"—a small sin with the potential to become a big one—so I made sure to tell Momma everything, even things that I'd promised my classmates I'd keep secret, like that John's older brother had shown him the sex scene in *Friday the 13th*, Kelly had stolen $5 from her mother's purse to buy candy bars, and Matt had forged his dad's signature on his behavioral report card. I wanted to have to confess as few things as possible to the priest, with the goal that he would consider me a "good" person and would relay that message to God. Although I hadn't seen Momma's journals, I could still sense that she was worried about something—she was more irritable than usual, she seemed to have less energy and expressed less excitement when I told her about my school day, and her hugs were longer and more frequent. I believed that if God thought I was "good," then he'd be able to make Momma healthy and keep my family safe.

On the day we were going to receive the Sacrament, my fourth-grade class lined up to confess our sins to a priest who was sitting in the corner of the church behind a portable screen. When it was my turn, I anxiously told the priest that I was jealous of how much attention my parents were giving my older sister, and I waited for him to say a prayer. Instead, he said, loudly, "I'm sorry, dear. I didn't hear you. Could you speak up?" I tried repeating my sin, but he interrupted my plea for forgiveness with a sneeze, and then he delivered a rushed prayer. "God forgives you," he said, and then added,

"You can signal for the next person in line." When I walked back to my pew, I thought of *The Wizard of Oz* and how I shouldn't trust people who hid behind screens, and I wondered what was so special about this priest that gave him the power to talk to God directly.

A barrier grew between God and me, a barrier that grew even bigger when Momma was diagnosed years later with breast cancer. The sicker she got, the less I cared about appealing to a God who was allowing it to happen—Momma's kind of malignancy didn't stem from any kind of sin. I cared about her approval, not God's.

Eventually, though, a barrier between Momma and me grew, too. The summer following my freshman year of college, I sat beside Momma's hospice bed, and as I gave her ice chips and applied more gauze to her wound, I felt an urgent need to have her "see" me. Even though I'd kept things from her so that she could focus on getting better instead of on the family's well-being, I still wanted her to know everything about me before it was too late. I wanted to confess that I'd lied to her about having a boyfriend, and that I'd made him up because I didn't want anyone to think that I was gay. I wanted her to be the first person to know that I really was gay. I wanted to tell her that I had a crush on my best female friend, and I wanted to know what she thought I should do about it. I wanted to tell her that I'd been feeling lost and lonely, and that I'd skipped several days of school for the first time in my life. I wanted to ask her what it felt like to really love someone. I wanted to confess that I'd lied to her when I said I was having a great time at college and was making a lot of new friends, and I wanted to confess that when I told her I was going to dorm parties, I was really in my own dorm room watching *Titanic* on loop, pausing it right before the ship hits the iceberg and then rewinding to the beginning. I wanted to tell her that because I was questioning both my sexuality and my belief in God, I felt out of place as a student at a large Catholic university. I wanted to admit that when I texted her from my campus that I was going for a swim, I was really going to the dining hall and binge eating until I felt better; that my dorm's resident assistant had written me a "warning letter" because I was crying too loudly in the common room one night after I'd gotten drunk by myself; that I was having trouble picking a major because I couldn't picture myself existing in the future; that I was having night terrors about her death. But as I watched Momma struggle to move, and I heard her whine from pain, my confessions seemed small, insignificant and selfish, so I said nothing instead.

During my time at college and my summer at home, Momma failed to confess certain things to me, too: the frequency of her emergency room trips and the duration of her hospital stays; the reason my dad was sleeping in the basement; the reasons she cried every night. We both avoided telling each other about wounds that weren't visible, our confessions remaining behind our screens.

*   *   *

When you walk into the rectory of Saint Pascal's Parish in Chicago, you'll see a small drawn rendering of Jesus. It's on top of parish brochures on a side table. It's a classic image of him—his skin is white, and he has long brown hair and a beard. The drawing cuts off at his neckline. He has brown eyes that are looking down—he looks sad, even a little lonely. It almost looks like a high school senior portrait, but one of the outtakes, the headshots parents don't bother to put in a nice frame or order in a larger size.

I'm sitting in a chair across from Jesus's picture as I wait for Father Thomas Dore to talk with me. After staring into Jesus's eyes for a few minutes, I start to feel sad for him. Maybe he got rejected from his top choice college. Or no one took him to prom. The atmosphere of the rectory makes me a little sad, too. It's monochromatic, each piece of furniture a light beige to match the walls, and I sit directly outside an office room. The office door is closed, but I can still overhear a priest complain to his rectory assistant that she shouldn't have scheduled him to preside over tomorrow's early morning baptism. I hear him sigh right before his assistant opens the door and walks past me. I look at the analog clock that hangs above Jesus. Father Dore is five minutes late.

I can't remember the first time I met Father Dore, but I must have been four or five years old. Father Dore was the pastor at St. Giles Catholic Parish for most of my grade school years, and he made a point of getting to know the families. He frequently came over to our house for dinner on Sunday nights, and after dinner he usually stayed for the new episode of *Malcolm in the Middle*—my whole family watched it together on the couch downstairs. Often, he fell asleep during the 30-minute episode, and Sarah (because the rest of us called "seniority" to get out of doing anything unpleasant) was charged with the task of waking him up. She tapped him gently on his shoulder, and if he didn't respond to that, she shook his shoulder with her hand.

Dore is now 81 years old and retired, and he walks toward me with a limp. Though the last time I saw him was nine years ago when he presided over Momma's funeral, he looks the same as I remember him—tall and confident, with a full head of white hair, a short, white beard, and glasses with tiny square frames. There are only a few differences in his appearance: he has a hearing aid in his left ear, and he isn't wearing a collar. He's wearing a navy blue button-down shirt with black dress pants, but even without the collar, his presence still intimidates me, and I'm worried about how he'll perceive me. I never spoke much to him when he visited our house, so even when he was at our dinner table, I still felt as distant from him as I did when he was at the altar and I was in the pew. I wonder if he expects that I still frequently attend church—he knows, from my dad, that I attended Notre Dame, so maybe he expects that the two of us will bond over our knowledge of Scripture. I pull down the right sleeve of my sweater to hide my forearm tattoo from him—I remember a religion teacher at St. Giles condemning tattoos as "impure and immoral"—and I smile widely at him as he apologizes for his lateness. He says it's his "off-day," so he was at the dentist—even though he's retired, he still frequently has tasks to perform, his "on-days." As he leads me into the room that the first priest and his assistant had exited, he apologizes for walking slowly. "Back problems," he says, and then laughs, "Comes with old age."

He didn't seem this physically weak on the day of Momma's funeral. He didn't have a limp; he walked steadily with purpose, and above her coffin, he held up the heavy Gospel without wavering.

Before we sit down in the meeting room, Dore hugs me, and his arms shake a little as he wraps them around me. His arms are as thin as a teenage girl's but without any muscle mass, just saggy skin. I wonder if the Gospel is too heavy for him to carry now. I don't want to put my arms all the way around him, fearing I will hurt him. It's an uncomfortable hug, like hugging the grandma on your dad's side, the one who always notices the stain on your shirt even when it's covered by a cardigan, on Christmas Eve—it seems mandatory although it comforts neither person, and even after it's over and you release, you still live in that hug for minutes afterward, her strong floral perfume sticking to your sweater.

Father Dore was a witness to Momma's suffering. He was at our house in her final days, praying beside her hospice bed and administering the Eucharist. It's typical for laypeople, or un-ordained clergy, to do this work, but Dore did it because he was so close to our family. The church refers to the administration of the Holy Eucharist to the sick as "Viaticum," meaning "food for the journey," with the idea that death is a journey into the afterlife. Anointing of the Sick is one of the two Sacraments of Healing—Reconciliation is the other—and it's performed to remind parishioners that when one person is sick, the entire community is wounded. I remember Father Dore's face as he laid the Eucharist on Momma's tongue—he didn't seem surprised by how sick Momma looked, or by the hospice attachments, and he didn't have pity in his eyes—he looked serious, certain and powerful, like he had a job to do, and he was going to finish it. I remember doubting, but still hoping, that his hands could heal her.

Even when I was younger, I don't think I ever felt absolutely sure that God existed. I couldn't picture him, so he seemed distant and unfamiliar. I never knew what to say to him, and when I did pray, it was a recitation—it seemed like a chore, and so did going to church every Sunday. Church involved constant repetition and didn't allow for much creativity— the service dictated our responses. "The Lord be with you," Father Dore would say, and everyone in the congregation would robotically respond, "And also with you." Although St. Giles cycled through a few cantors per year, they all sang the same songs each Sunday, and they all had raspy, untrained voices. One cantor was completely tone-deaf, and my sisters and I would groan when we saw her walk up to the microphone for the responsorial psalm on her assigned Sundays. I prayed before I went to bed each night when I was in grade school, but instead of saying the "Our Father," I usually just asked for things and waited to see if I got them the next day. I asked for things like extra candy in my lunch, an "I love you" note from a grade-school crush, and an "A" on a math test, and I saw God as just one big disappointment when I didn't get anything I asked for.

I craved the certainty that Father Dore seemed to have. Whenever he gave a homily, his voice boomed throughout the church. The boom was like an imperative—I always interpreted it as, "Follow my message ... or else"—and I re-member being scared by it. I wanted to hide under the pew to escape it. Instead, many Sundays, the children of the congre-gation were called up to the altar to sit around Father Dore as he delivered his homily, and he directed it specifically at us. He would look at each kid and say, "You are God's chosen one." Other times he'd wag his finger at one of us and warn, "Listen to your parents." Because I was a quiet, nervous, and insecure kid, a loud voice, to me, indicated a level of "truth"— the louder the voice, the truer the words.

In the same 1998 journal, Momma wrote:

My white blood cell count is higher, but not frighteningly so. My thyroid is probably the cause of my recent exhaustion; I'll pick up the prescription tomorrow.

For a religion assignment, Meaghan and I talked about what God means to me. She really seemed to understand my explanation, and as part of the assignment, put it into words and an abstract collage about water. It was great art and a real pleasure that she understood what I said.

Was Momma's God like water, something tangible but not a "person"? Did her idea of God change as she got sick or closer to death? I wonder if Father Dore, as he put the Eucharist to her lips, could gauge her degree of certainty about God, or if he could sense what she thought about life after death.

"Many things are blurry about when my mom was in hospice," I say to him, my voice a bit shaky, as we sit across from each other, "but I remember your face. I remember you being there." He nods and then says, "You know, dealing with the

issues of health and death is the hardest part of being a priest."
He runs his fingers through his beard, like he's thinking carefully about what to say next. His homilies always lasted longer
than the other priests, but he rarely repeated things—he was,
and still is, judicious in his word choice and precise about the
message he wants to get across. He says, "Your mother's funeral is on the list of top three most difficult ones over which
I've presided." It's second, he says, after the Barnett baby,
Paige, who died at 18 months from a "lightning-quick inva-
sion" of *Streptococcus pneumoniae*. Keith Barnett, Paige's dad,
had gone to wake Paige up from her nap and found her lying
in her crib, blue. Ranking third is the funeral of Father Dore's
close friend, whose name he doesn't say, who died abruptly
in a car accident.

I'm a little taken aback that he's ranked Momma's funeral
"second." I remember him saying, quietly, "I'll help if I can,"
when I called to ask about meeting for our interview. Maybe
he feels that he won't be helpful to me if he doesn't express
how much Momma's death affected him. But I wonder about
his relationship to her. I don't remember it being particularly special. She sometimes laughed at him for falling asleep
during *Malcolm in the Middle,* and she frequently comment-
ed on his bad table manners—he used to clink his silverware
together a few times before cutting up the food on his plate.
Dore was always much closer to my dad. The two of them still
get together every once in a while—they go out to dinner,

movies, or sporting events. Why would Momma's funeral rank above Dore's close friend's? But as I stare at him from across the room, I think about the peace that certainty must bring, and I stop myself from asking him why he feels this way. I choose, instead, for the first time since grade school, to take his word for it.

Dore shifts from the topic of health and death to his role as a retired pastor. He talks about the different religious retreats he's gone to in his retirement and about his daily activities within the church. He says he periodically helps out at both St. Pascal and St. Giles, delivering the occasional homily, listening to parishioners' confessions, and talking one-on-one with parishioners who have specific concerns or who are having crises in faith. But his knees are weak, so he can't kneel during the Communion rite, and even standing for prolonged periods is painful for him, so recently he's been getting fewer calls to help out.

He grew up down the street from St. Pascal, and he says that it "feels funny" to be back in this neighborhood after so many years. He talks about his childhood—his parents' involvement in the church and their role in his "faith journey." Both of his parents were very active in the church, and at a young age, Dore became an altar server. Ever since he was a kid, he felt that one day he would have a big role in the church, he says. He talks about his seminary training at Quigley Preparatory in downtown Chicago, and how at home he felt there. "I knew that the Lord wanted me," he says, "and he was calling me home. I felt his presence, and I thought, 'I'm not going to argue with him.'"

As Dore talks about his relationship to God, I realize that part of me feels desperate to relate to him, like I'm a child who wants her parents' approval and consolation. I can't explain exactly why, but I want Dore to like me. Maybe there's a part of me that still believes he can relay my "goodness" to God, and that God could grant me happiness. There's still a part of me that hopes I'm wrong to be skeptical of God's existence.

After a brief silence, Dore decides it's his turn to ask me questions. When he asks about the Chicago neighborhood, Edgewater, where I live, and how often I go to church, I'm afraid to tell him that I stopped going a long time ago. I stutter and then mumble something about not knowing if there was even a church by me. He raises an eyebrow and then asks about my cross street. When I answer, he says, "There's a church right by you, right on Broadway. The old gothic one. It's right there." When I respond with, "Oh, that's right," he gives me a strange look, then rests his chin between his thumb and index finger and says, "I think you're overdue for a homily."

The boom begins. It feels even more overwhelming in this small room, just the two of us. He has different concerns today than he had during the old homilies I remember: "We're getting and receiving, and we're not focused on giving," he says. "It's all, 'Buy this now at a cheaper price.' It's bigger this, bigger that—a bigger bed, a bigger car, a bigger phone—stuff to make you look better and nicer." He looks down for a minute at my iPhone 7, which is recording the interview from the table between us. "Do we really need the iPhone 7?" he asks. "What happens to it all when there's the next big thing? It winds up in your attic, or your basement, or your storage unit. Where does our faith come in?"

He continues, "People try to find meaning in things like sex, fame, and money, but what they really need is God." He talks about drug and alcohol addiction as a misplaced longing for God, and then he adds, "Suicide is a longing, too. People long to stop feeling empty, so they turn to sinful things."

As he says this, I picture Tammy, the nurse who'd been assigned to me after my overdose, handing me a Styrofoam cup filled with charcoal and saying, "Drink this. It will save your life." She stared at me as I stared down at the charcoal: a black residue, ash-like and porous, the remains of the campfire I attended in the woods when I was sixteen and drunk for the first time the night after Momma had a double mastectomy; the blackness at the bottom of the bowl that I used to smoke weed before a school presentation because, as I told myself, it worked better than anti-anxiety medications; the thickness of the cement parking spot in the alley where my first girlfriend and I carved our names, not just as an act of rebellion but also a chance to declare ourselves as a gay couple, carving our identities to feel more at ease with them; the black ink that the tattoo artist wiped off my forearm as he finished Max's crown from Maurice Sendak's *Where the Wild Things Are*, a book Momma used to read to me when I was little. Hours later, long after I'd thrown out the empty cup, I rushed to the bathroom—a side-effect of charcoal consumption—and vomited up what took me so long to get down, a long and huge release, a vomit so uncontainable that it sprayed in a web-like pattern over the toilet bowl and stool, black matter zigzagging and striping the white seat, expelling death and creating a mess of memory.

Dore pauses his homily, and we sit in silence for a moment as I study him. He looks lonely, and there's a kind of desperation about him. Maybe he's needed someone to talk to for a while. Maybe he's sad or even depressed, living in a small room in a rectory where, eventually, maybe even soon, he'll die. Most days he just sits with his thoughts. I get the sense from our interview that he communicates every once in a while with his sister, but he has no other living family and only a few friends. He doesn't have a personal phone, and he doesn't use the Internet. He considers my dad a close friend, and he says he's marked on his calendar when they're next going out for dinner—but that's eight weeks from now. He's missed having an audience, I think.

I wonder what he longs for. I wonder, too, what he isn't confessing to me, and I wonder if he avoids thinking about some aspects of health and death because they threaten his certainty. Does he get anxious, too? Does he stay up at night, unable to shut off his mind? Is he able to acknowledge some of the contradictions in the church's doctrine? I wonder if he's ever seen *The Wizard of Oz*, and I wonder if he felt sad, like I did, when Dorothy finds out that the Wizard is just an ordinary old man.

As Father Dore's voice fades to the background, the voices of my memories increase, and I think more about the things that Momma and I didn't say to each other and the moment her body was wheeled out of the bedroom. I prayed to God when she was in hospice. I apologized to him for neglecting prayer for years, but once again I was asking him for something—Momma's life. And again, he didn't deliver. But in the moments before Momma's death, even after my dad had administered the morphine and she was incoherent, I'd convinced myself that she'd get better. I told myself that she wouldn't die, over and over again, until it sounded true.

I feel my face growing hotter with the anger that I still harbor about her death, and my desire to impress Father Dore begins to fade. Where was his God when Momma, at age 52, was lowered into the ground? Where was God when my 15-year-old sister watched as Momma was carried out of the house in a body bag? Many of the adults at Momma's wake told me that she would always be with me, but when I pray to her, she doesn't answer. I scream at the silence.

Each June, on the anniversary of her death, my family returns to Queen of Heaven cemetery, and we sit on the grass
beside her grave. We say, "Hi, we miss you." I don't believe
anymore that the shining sun is her saying "hi" back, and I
don't believe that, like Jesus, she'll rise from the dead. Father
Dore's Eucharist didn't do anything to heal her.

I think of Jesus after he's condemned to death, his back
covered with lashes, his head crowned with thorns, carrying a
heavy cross on his bruised shoulders. I think of the huge nails
hammered through his hands and feet. He bleeds heavily, his
arms outstretched, his believers witnesses to the horror of it
all. I prayed for a miracle, and instead there was just that cross,
and all that blood.

I can feel sweat dripping down my face as my mind flashes the events of my freshman year in college—the frequency
of gay bashings on campus, the sociology professor who was
fired by the university president for coming out to a fellow
professor as a gay man, the DVDs of *The L Word* that I hid
under my pillow so that my roommate wouldn't find them,
Momma in the Maywood hospital after a bad infection, the
cancer spreading throughout her body, the day I received the
news that she would soon have to be under hospice care. I
think about how, to Father Dore, my gayness is not visible
like a tattoo, and I wonder if he can see the rage in my eyes.

I grow bolder in my anger, which makes it easier for me

to ask him the following question: "You said earlier that my mother's funeral was really difficult for you. Did it change your relationship to God?" He stares at me for a moment, and he looks puzzled, so I try to clarify. "I mean, are there ever times when you've questioned whether or not God actually exists?"

He responds to my question with a story about a parishioner who, after visiting his mother, a late-stage dementia patient in a nursing home, had asked Dore, "Why me?" Dore's response was, "Why not you? Why do you think you're exempt from hardship?" God never promised us that terrible things wouldn't happen, he says, before a loud exhale. But then Dore's tone shifts, becoming softer and more solemn, as he confesses, "I was angry at God when my mother died." He continues, looking down at the floor:

> My favorite song from the church used to be "Be Not Afraid." The band played it for my 25th anniversary in the church, and also for my 40th anniversary. But then my mom died some years after that, and they played it at her funeral. So I won't listen to it again. Right before she died, she had fear in her eyes. She was very afraid to die.

His own eyes widen as he talks about his mother's fear, and I remember something I'd briefly forgotten about Momma's funeral.

Momma requested all female pallbearers—postmortem feminism. My dad, sisters, and I stood before the church's entrance behind them. Father Dore stood in front of the pallbearers (Momma's "network of moms" from the St. Giles and Oak Park community) and her casket, but he faced us instead of looking forward toward the altar. The pianist began playing "On Eagle's Wings," and the cantor waited for a cue to start singing the first verse. The music must have played for just about 30 seconds before my dad had to excuse himself to cry in the church bathroom, to the right of where we were standing. When my dad exited the bathroom, his eyes were red. Dore looked at my dad's eyes, and as soon as he knew my dad had been crying, he began crying, too. Then my sisters and I cried, too, as we trailed behind Momma's raised casket down the altar while "On Eagle's Wings" continued to play.

As we advanced toward the altar, Father Dore was crying, but he also looked worried, or scared. He seemed unsure.

Now, as he looks straight at me instead of down at the floor, Dore talks more about his own mother's death. He doesn't say more about his anger—just what relieves him of it. "When I'm angry, I find it's best for me to have a routine," he says. His routine involves taking flowers to his mother's grave on the anniversary of her death. "And I just talk to her," he says.

When I look into Father Dore's eyes this time, they don't

look rigid or judging like they did when I was in grade school. Instead, they look weary—his eyes remind me of Momma's eyes after her double mastectomy—and like his mother before her death, there is some fear in them. His eyes look like the eyes of an 81-year-old man, but also like the eyes of a child. He's tired from all of his experiences, but maybe he's also newly seeing, or still seeking.

Referring to God and the stories of the Bible, Dore admits that every once in a while, when he's praying, he thinks to himself, "Is this shit real?" We laugh together, the sincere kind of laughter, and at this moment I realize that Father Dore is not wiser than the rest of society, nor is he otherworldly. He's just trying to figure out how to exist.

I think that losing a parent even at an old age places a person, at least temporarily, back in the role of a neglected, confused child. As I watch Father Dore, I realize that I long for something from God that's impossible for me to get. I want to curl up in a ball and lean my head on God's shoulders while he shushes me and tells me everything will be all right. I want God to sing me to sleep. In the morning I want him to tell me to get up and make my bed. I want him to tell me that I'm irritable because I'm not eating enough, and then I want him to say, "Check the cabinets. I just bought some Rice Krispy Treats." I want him to tell me that he talked to my sisters and my dad and he comforted them, too. I want him to hold our family together. I want him to hear me play the trumpet and tell me that I'm talented and that he's so proud of me.

"You leave your clothes on the floor, you leave your towel on the floor, you leave your books and laptop throughout the house, you are cranky in the morning, you are noisy late at night, yet each time you leave here to return to college, I'm as sad as the first time." That's what I want God to say. "I miss you," I want him to say. "Everything is O.K.; you are strong; you are smart; you are beautiful; I'm trying to figure out how to get an AIM screen name so I can iChat with you; do your homework; go to class; stop swearing; Caitlin Hogan Garvey, I am so mad at you; call in and check when you get to Katie's house; stop shaving your eyebrows or you'll start to look like Whoopi Goldberg; you really need to get a haircut; remember to take your vitamins; I love you."

I want God to wear white polo shirts and khakis when it's Sunday before church and he's getting the paper and Krispy Kreme donuts for my sisters and me—he doesn't eat any, he has a grapefruit instead. I want him to cheer too loudly at my swim meet. I want him to visit seven different Hallmarks trying to find the Princess Diana Bear Beanie Baby for my Easter basket. I want him to throw a spoon at me when he's mad at me for something stupid I said. I want him to buy a Halloween costume for our dog. But I don't want him at all. I'm scared, and I want my Momma.

Without Momma, I think I'll always feel a degree of uncertainty—I can't know for sure what she felt as she was dying, and I can't know if/when I'll feel relieved of my depression. A few months after Momma died, I went to a fortune-teller in Oak Park. I hoped she would see a future that I couldn't. After looking at her tarot cards, she told me that she saw a tall, dark man as my future husband, and that I should call my mother more often.

I remember someone saying to me, "I guess even the best doctors couldn't perform a miracle," on the day of Momma's funeral.

I remember my grandma's sister, "a fat Betty Boop," she called herself, as she finished gluing on her fake eyelashes and then sat down to read my palms, her manicured fingers tickling the creases of my skin and her scratchy voice saying, "Well, sweet child, it looks to me like you'll live a long, long time."

*   *   *

As my dad got ready to drive me to my college orientation, I said goodbye to Momma in 2007 at the end of August. It was then, as I hugged her, that I realized that she and my dad probably hadn't told me everything. I could feel it in her hug—that no matter the treatment, she was going to die, and the two of them had known that for a while. Momma was not big on physical affection in part because hugs were painful for her, but when we hugged before I loaded my last suitcase into my dad's car, I thought it might never end. She was crying—sobbing, really—and our bodies were shaking as we held onto each other. She was squeezing me, and it must have been hurting her. I didn't want to leave, but I knew she would never let me stay.

I'd only seen Momma cry once before that, on the day her dad died. And I only saw her cry once after that, when she was in hospice, high on morphine, and insisting that her dad was there, in her bedroom.

I cried through the two hours it took for my dad to drive to South Bend, even when he stopped at McDonalds to get us McFlurries. When we got to Notre Dame, his alma mater, I asked him if we could just sit on a bench for a while. Because he put his enthusiasm for showing me his favorite parts of campus on the back burner, I knew that he was feeling many of the same things that I was. We sat in silence on that bench together, as happy freshmen walked by us with new student IDs around their necks and shower caddies in grocery bags around their wrists.

CHAPTER FOUR

The Hospice Nurse

On a Tuesday morning in January, my kindergarten class was going to the moon. I knew about rockets, and I was thrilled for the adventure. I didn't feel fully prepared for the journey since we hadn't learned much about it in class, but this didn't matter to me; at age four, I was ready to get away from it all. The Monday before, I prepared my outfit. I imagined the moon might be cold, so I laid out my puffy pink coat and snow pants. Momma told me not to forget my Velcro boots and my helmet, and she packed a lunch for me, too. I remember thinking that she'd never know if I didn't finish my apple on the moon. On the day of the mission, she dropped me off at school, and I hugged her and said, "I'll get in touch with you as soon as I can."

I showed up to school in my moon outfit, and Mrs. Mamolella ushered our class outside. "The moon is in the playground," she said, before adding, "Make sure to zip up your jackets." I went outside with the other kids, and I looked around for our rocket. It wasn't there. Instead, there was a cardboard moon taped to the fence. There were no rockets, just tricycles, and we were supposed to take turns riding our tricycles to the cardboard moon, navigating in and out of cones. And to make matters worse, many of our parents were already standing near the cardboard moon with their cameras. Momma was smiling and waving, and I frowned back at her and hoped she could see it. How could they do this to us? Momma had just circled the block after dropping me off, but she'd let me think that I was going to space. I'd estimated we'd be gone for at least a week, and I thought I could float away—I wouldn't have to drink the gross milk we got every day for afternoon snack; I wouldn't have to "speak up" or "be social," like Mrs. Mamolella always told me to do; I wouldn't have to get all my chores done before playing outside. I could jump high and say goodbye to my classmates forever if I wanted.

I was not at all in the mood to play pretend, but I've never liked confrontation, so I rode my tricycle in my moon outfit and Velcro boots, navigating through the orange cones, to the uninspired cardboard. I didn't smile when Momma said, "Sweetie, look at the camera," but I looked up and furrowed my brows for the click, making sure that she knew I was mad at her while still letting her document the day.

After my turn on the tricycle was over, I asked my best friend, John, if he was upset, too. He said, "Why? Did you think we were going to the real one?" I didn't answer, and I realized that I was not only disappointed, but also gullible. Everyone else seemed to understand reality and its limitations. I wondered why all the cool things were lies. Santa Claus was a fraud, and so was the Tooth Fairy—Momma accidentally woke my sister Meaghan up when she was putting a dollar under her pillow, and Meaghan whispered the truth to me one night after dinner—and Momma's bruises weren't goodnight kisses from the moon. One night, while pressing my ear up against my parents' bedroom door, I overheard my dad saying he was concerned about the bruises and that he and Momma should go to the doctor.

I was 18 when one of the hospice nurses sat us down in the living room on the night before Momma died and said, "Your mother likely only has one night left. But when she goes, she will go in peace." She talked about heaven and how Momma would ultimately feel relief. My mother deserved heaven, the hospice nurse said, especially after all those years of pain. I remember wanting to laugh. I didn't, just to be respectful, but I thought, "What does this lady know?" I stared at her clipboard of notes, her purple scrubs, her file filled with Momma's health history, and I listened to the clicking of her pen and never looked her in the eye. She didn't belong in our home. She was just full of false information, cynical with age, and her pessimism about Momma's lifespan was making the house feel claustrophobic, like a coffin. She was closing the lid. I wanted to scream at her to leave.

Maybe I should have been skeptical of Momma instead, who kept saying, despite lying in that hospice bed, that she felt better, that she was probably healing and she'd soon have the strength to get up on her own. Momma's health was the moon. We couldn't actually reach it. There were artificial signs of progress—one day, suddenly, her appetite returned, and we cheered, and we exhaled, just for a moment, before remembering that this was terminal, that rockets were just tricycles, and that no amount of pedaling could blast us off into space.

The hospice nurse was right. Momma died the next day. It took me months to believe. It was a different kind of skepticism. The kind that protects.

*   *   *

The patients of hospice nurses die. Some, very quickly. I was curious to find out how these nurses perform their jobs, witnessing death maybe multiple times a day and traveling from patient to patient while having to maintain a pleasant demeanor. How could any human sustain this career? I wondered if it requires a certain personality—someone exceptionally strong-willed and resilient. After Momma died and I was back on the Notre Dame campus for my sophomore year, I signed up to volunteer for a hospice organization in South Bend. Being a volunteer didn't require any special training—my only task was to be present, to show up and sit in the chair next to my assigned patients, chatting with them if they were awake, and playing cards with them or reading out loud to them if they felt like it. I thought this would help me with the stage of grief in which I felt stuck: denial. On my first day of volunteering, I sat for a few hours next to Oliver, a sleeping 90-year-old patient with liver disease, and I did some homework while listening to the consistent rhythm of his breathing. He slept with a slight smile on his face, and I felt calm for the first time in a while. His breathing was a song, and I felt tied to him, like we had a silent understanding, making each other stronger through our subtle smiles. Early the next morning, the hospice administrator called me to say that Oliver had died in his sleep. I never went back.

I think I would rather be one of those ice road truckers, performing under life-threatening physical conditions and measuring success through survival, than have a career as a hospice nurse. I'd rather experience the cold highway hypnosis of the Arctic Circle, trucking my heavy cargo over a thin layer of ice that was never meant to be a road, than stand near the bed, with all those tubes in that master bedroom, when the wife's face distorts from horror as she holds her husband's hand and realizes, for the first time in her life, what it means for a body to grow cold.

I asked my dad for the name of the hospice organization that Momma's hospital had selected for her. He said it was called Heartland Hospice, and I started my research. On their website, they boast of being the third-largest provider in the nation, delivering care in 23 states. I called, as well as emailed, the Heartland that serves Cook County, or more specifically, that served Momma in her last months in our Oak Park home, but I received no response. After trying a few more times, I decided, instead, to email the next closest Heartland—in Rockford, Illinois, about 1.5 hours from Oak Park—to see if a nurse there would be interested in talking to me. Although it was extremely unlikely that one of the hospice nurses that had met Momma would now be working at the Rockford location, I figured any nurse's story could answer my questions about this career path. In my email, I clarified that I was not expecting to speak with the nurse or team who worked with Momma.

Within a few minutes, Pamela Weiss, the Rockland Heartland administrator, emailed back, telling me to please call her "Pam." Pam wrote that she was excited to meet me at her Rockford office and that she'd call me upon her return from the Annual Assembly of Hospice and Palliative Care in Phoenix.

*   *   *

The car ride from Chicago takes almost two hours, and I drive past several orchards and farms to reach the Heartland office. It's an unassuming brown brick building, low and flat with a few shrubs near the front door. For the most part, Heartland looks like an average work environment—Pam has her own office next to a conference room, and down the narrow hallway, there's a small cafeteria and a few desks with computers. Several young nurses in scrubs are sitting in front of computers. They don't seem to be using the screens—instead, they are laughing and chatting, and one nurse is heating up some food in the microwave. It all seems strangely cheerful, and I almost forget why I'm there.

I pick up what I think is a brochure from the side table next to my chair, and upon opening it, I realize that it's actually a donation envelope, the kind that gets tucked into Bibles in church pews. The cover image is of a young white woman in a fancy dress, who is holding the hand of a small boy with her left hand while her right hand is fully stretched toward the sky. Together they look up at the white balloon that the woman has just released. She looks relieved to be letting the balloon go, watching it float higher and higher, eager to see it disappear behind the clouds. "Your gift makes a difference," the second page reads. "It will enable children, teens, and adults to attend grief camps, where they can spend invaluable time with others who are also starting the healing process." Toward the bottom of the page, in italics, there's an anecdote from Ralph, "retired police officer and grief camp attendee," who, despite having initial doubts about grief camp being "his thing," expresses gratitude for the peace it gave him—he exclaims, "I can't believe how great this program was for me!"

I wonder how Ralph feels about being labeled a "grief camp attendee." I imagine him releasing his white balloon, the other grief camp attendees next to him in the grass, all gently smiling on the verge of the release of their own balloons. I picture the balloons rising together, some bumping into each other, floating toward forgotten.

I tuck the envelope into my bag as two women walk through the front doors. I don't recognize either of them—one is tall and thin with short brown hair, and she looks to be middle aged, and the other is shorter and younger looking, her blonde hair pulled back into a ponytail. The receptionist looks at them and nods in my direction. "Oh, my God!" Pam, the brown-haired one, says when she sees me. "I'm so glad you're here." As soon as I stand up, she hugs me. It's like we've been lifelong friends. I'm not normally a big fan of physical contact with someone I've just met, but earlier, a few minutes before I walked into Heartland, I swallowed three Klonopin tablets that I'd remembered to stuff in my backpack. I have high levels of anxiety whenever I'm introduced to someone for the first time: my heart races, my face turns red, I stutter and forget words, my forehead drips with sweat, and my shoulders shrug around my neck. But the physical effects of my social anxiety are even more unbearable when I'm meeting someone who is exceptionally friendly and enthusiastic. Even though we'd only communicated via email, I sensed Pam would fit these characteristics, and I came prepared. Klonopin turns me into a chattier and bubblier person. It allows me to perfect the art of "fake nice." The tablets warm my stomach and tingle my face, so I smile widely at Pam and the woman accompanying her. I usually take a maximum of two Klonopin tablets at once, and the third one, I quickly realize, has made me slightly high.

Another hug. This one from the blonde-haired woman. It's more of a squeeze, and when she releases, I notice she's tearing up a bit. I'm still grinning. Pam says, "Caitlin, you won't believe this," and she touches the other woman on the shoulder. "This is Abby," Pam says, and then adds, "She's worked at the Rockford Heartland for many years." Then, Abby speaks up. "I'm so happy to see you here, Caitlin," she says. "I was one of the nurses who took care of your mom."

I can feel my smile morph into a sort of snarl, and the Klonopin is making my facial muscles feel heavy, and it's clear that my upper lip won't be able to snap out of its snarl any time soon. Abby takes out a tissue from the pocket of her jeans and wipes her eyes. "Breast cancer. Three young girls," she says, shaking her head in what appears to be sadness and disbelief. "I was there."

Abby begins to describe what she remembers of my child-hood home. "I can picture it vividly," she says, before rattling off from her memory map: "Your house was on a quiet cul-de-sac, a long one-story brick home, with an open layout inside, the bedroom adjacent to the kitchen, and, if I'm remember-ing correctly, there was a kitchen island—(two-second pause as she closes her eyes to better visualize)—yes! Definitely! There was definitely a kitchen island. And a snack bar, too. That was a neat snack bar. What else? Oh! Vaulted ceilings!"

Abby seems thrilled with herself. She's smiling, and Pam's smiling, and I'm still snarling, but they don't notice, and Pam says to me, "Can you believe what an amazing memory Abby has?"

I giggle at the question. Despite a three-tablet Klonopin high, my anxiety hasn't completely subsided, and when I feel uncomfortable, I tend to laugh, often at inappropriate times. Pam and Abby stare at me, waiting for me to say something. I laugh again, harder this time, and I can feel my face turning red. Pam and Abby exchange glances, the judging kind that indicates their uneasiness. Their glances, combined with the inappropriateness of my laughter, make the situation even funnier to me, and I'm not sure I'll be able to keep myself from laughing a third time.

My sisters and I refer to any inappropriate laughter as "church laughter," and for a fleeting moment it's 1998 again. My family and I are sitting in the front pew during Sunday mass at Saint Giles. Meaghan has just whispered something to

Sarah and me that's caused the three of us to burst out laughing during the usually silent Eucharistic prayer. Momma, sitting to the right of us, whips her head to the left and glares at us, but since she's turned to the side, her ear is now close enough for Sarah to whisper the joke to her, too. Momma laughs, gently at first, and then, suddenly, she begins crying from laughter, a full-body laugh, tossing her head back and shaking her shoulders, her loud laughter enveloping the hollow church. This causes my dad to start laughing, too, even though he hasn't heard the joke. My dad coughs sometimes when he laughs too hard, and his cough-laugh joins our guffaws and echoes down the pews. The five of us have accidentally recreated the Uncle Albert scene from *Mary Poppins*, levitating with laughter despite a surrounding silence, and at that moment, I hope that, like Albert, it will take at least three days for someone to get us down from the ceiling. A few weeks from then, none of us will even remember the initial joke, but we will laugh, all over again, about that scene. We will remember the rush of roaring through a silent ritual, and we will remember the weightlessness of a body that's been temporarily freed from worry, and we will find ourselves longing, always, for that feeling's return.

My mind flashes the image of the white balloon on the cover of the Heartland donation envelope. It tugs me back to the present. I try to collect myself. As I stand facing Abby and Pam, a few things are clear to me:

1. Except for the "Breast cancer. Three young girls" comment, every single thing that Abby said was incorrect. I did not live in a long, low home on a quiet cul-de-sac, and although I would have delighted in a snack bar, my parents would never have entertained that idea. We lived in an old three-story brick house, across the street from a park. My parents' bedroom was on the second floor, and the kitchen was on the first. The rooms of our house were clearly designated, separated by walls, and our ceilings weren't vaulted.

2. It is possible to abruptly snap out of a three-tablet Klonopin high, although it might require meeting someone who is under the false impression that she was your dead mother's caretaker.

3. No longer under the pleasant high of anti-anxiety medication, I will not have the courage nor the heart to tell Abby that her memory, in fact, is not that amazing: she has explained the living situation of a completely different Denise Garvey. Or, more likely, the patient Abby is thinking about was not named Denise Garvey at all. Abby's patient lived in Rockford, the only Heartland location where Abby has worked. To give Abby the benefit of the doubt, it is possible that there was a second Denise Garvey, a Rockford resident with three young girls, who, nine years ago, was also dying from inflammatory breast cancer, the kind that accounts for just one percent of all breast cancer cases in the United States, and who was under Abby's care.

4. This is my first time in Rockford, and it will likely also be my last. I'm not sure if my parents have ever visited Rockford. More importantly, though, if I'm not able to tell Abby that she has my family mixed up with one of her other patients, then I will be validating her truth.

I try to pull myself together. This woman has already hugged me, and she's already visualized that old cul-de-sac. In return, I've essentially laughed in her face. Who am I to tell her that her truth has nothing to do with mine? I choose my words carefully enough so that later, when I transcribe the taped conversation, I won't entirely hate myself for blatantly lying. "I'm so sorry for laughing," I say to Abby. "It's just that you completely took me by surprise. It's crazy! I can't believe it. I wasn't expecting to speak with anyone who was on my mother's care-taking team. I am so grateful to see you, and I can't thank you enough for the work that you do for Heartland." Abby begins to cry again, and Pam gives me a second hug. "We're so lucky you're here," Pam says.

Abby then explains to me that she'd only come to the office today to see me and to make sure she got the chance to tell me about her role in Momma's care. She has to leave shortly for a home visit to one of her patients. My visit was inconvenient for Abby's work schedule, but still she showed up, bringing the memories of a patient with her, just not the memories of my actual mother. Maybe she needed some sort of validation from me. Hospice work seems lonely, and based on Pam's reaction to my visit, I imagine very few family members of hospice patients reach out to the nurses, after everything settles down, to thank them or to just talk with them. Maybe Abby even realized, at some point in our interaction, that she was mistaken. Did we both play pretend for the other's sake?

Abby has a huge smile on her face, and her mascara is smeared over her damp eyelids. As I watch her walk out of Heartland, I wonder if it even matters that our memories are incompatible. Abby had a patient once who had breast cancer, and Momma had a hospice nurse. We were witnesses to the same kind of suffering, a body's slow collapse. I start to cry a little, too, when Abby disappears from my sight.

As the front doors close behind Abby, Pam signals me into her office, and just as we're about to sit down for our interview, she says, "There are just some patients we will never forget. Your mom was one of those patients." And suddenly, once again, I can feel myself levitating toward Uncle Albert's ceiling.

*   *   *

Sarah once asked me if I'd ever pretended that Momma didn't actually die, that she just faked the whole thing somehow. Maybe it was all a show, and she was just fed up with

her current life—motherhood and marriage—and she started over somewhere, *tabula rasa*. Once, after she died, I saw
Momma in the dairy section of the grocery store, scanning
cartons for cracked eggs. She was wearing a polo shirt and
high-waisted jeans, and her blonde hair was still cut short, but
it was thick and shiny, and it looked healthy. When she finally chose an egg carton and swung around to place it in her
cart, I could see her full face with its unfamiliar features, and
Momma had vanished. Sarah's idea gave me comfort, though,
this belief in a different reality.

Now, I sit on the chair across from Pam, who sits behind
the computer screen at her desk. She's wearing a red and
white polka dot shirt that's covered by a cardigan. Her brown
hair is in a bob, and she's wearing black eyeliner. She's small
and skinny, but she looks tough, like she's constantly active
or buzzing around. Her desk and office walls display framed
photographs of her family—in the picture on her desk, she's
smiling with her daughter, their arms draped around each other. Her desk is home to a big stack of paperwork. She opens
her desk drawer to show me the journals that she keeps—in
them, she writes down her work stresses and her observa-
tions of other hospice nurses, she says. Her voice is nasally,
but soothing, like a therapist's, and she's smiling widely as
she tells me about her background and how she ended up
at Heartland. After high school, she says, she enlisted in the

military. She had a job as a med-tech, so she worked in the obstetrics department at the age of 18, helping doctors deliver babies. "Wow," I respond, "that must have been a tough transition, from bringing life into the world to the world of hospice." But she tells me that it didn't feel like much of a change at all. Death and life, she says, are two intimate areas. She explains:

> When you have your gallbladder removed, so what? But when you deliver a baby, you do not forget those people, the nurses, the doctors, and the patients. I vividly remember my room for each of my own deliveries, my two daughters. But I just had toe surgery in December, and I don't know who took care of me or what room I was in. Birth and death are times you don't ever forget. Nobody's the boss except for that baby, who is calling the shots. And that's Heartland's philosophy—meet people where they're at and let them call the shots. I always tell patients we're all on the same bus. You are in the driver's seat, and your family is in the first and second rows, I'll say to them, and all of the nurses are behind you.

There's something about the way she says that last line that reminds me of group therapy in South Bend. The main therapist led the wheels of the bus round and round, and when the bus picked us up we were supposed to say something profound about our character. Moving his arms up and down in a circular manner, the therapist said, "And we're rolling!" and then he stopped on Diane. Diane was a recovering drug addict with an eating disorder who always said "pass" when the therapist asked her about her father. "Yesterday I cried after eating a bite of pizza," Diane said. "But I did it. I finished it." And we resumed rolling. The bus tried to pick me up next. I looked at the therapist and then mumbled, "Um, I don't know what to say." The bus came to a screeching halt.

The inside of Heartland reminds me a little of the psychiatric facility, too. When Pam pauses our interview after her lengthy discussion of her role as an administrator, she takes me into what she calls the "Good Thoughts Room." A wreath hangs on the wall, but instead of pine cones within its leaves, there are the names of patients on slips of colored paper. There are hundreds of names, and there are pictures of the patients surrounding the wreath. There's a fuzzy white rug on the floor underneath the wreath, a beanbag chair in the corner, and a few unlit candles on a small wooden desk across from the beanbag chair. "This is where we relax, meditate, and just think about our patients. We picture them in a happier place," Pam says. The room looks like Room 375, my inpatient assignment, and it has the same atmosphere. Despite the modern décor, Good Thoughts Room still feels like a hospital room, its headache-inducing fluorescent lights and cold floor tiles around the rug. Somehow, it smells like a hospital, too: hand sanitizer and sickness. Something about it seems false, even intentionally deceptive, covering up sterility with scented candles.

On Valentine's Day in group therapy, we wrote our names on paper hearts, and the art therapist strung them all together and hung them on the wall. The red string was short—it only needed to hold our seven names—and it was lopsided. I looked at our names on the hearts: Caitlin, Ivan, Diane, Ross, Sandy, James, and Katherine. I'd never felt more alone.

Pam shows me the prayer room, which is across from the Good Thoughts Room. There's a crucifix on the center wall, though Heartland is not affiliated with a particular religion. Heartland has social workers, chaplains, and bereavement counselors, who help the nurses "focus on feelings." Pam explains that the availability of these services distinguishes hospice nursing from other fields: "There's a study that shows oncology nurses burn out faster than hospice nurses," she says, "because they are so focused on healing. When their patients die, they don't have anywhere to vent."

Pam believes that different nursing fields require different personalities, an observation she made in her years between serving in the military and working at Heartland. In those years, she worked as an oncology nurse at Saint Anthony's in Rockford. She enjoyed the work, but when a nurse practitioner told her more about hospice care and said she'd be

a good fit, she decided to make the transition. "E.R. nurses move quickly. It's all about emergency for them," Pam
explains. "They just go, go, go, and you can't get a word in.
They are always wired, always anticipating." Surgery nurses,
on the other hand, are "intense, constantly focused, serious,"
and they don't take time to socialize. "And then you'll see
the hospice nurses," Pam laughs, "and we're just sitting at the
lunch table for, like, three hours, talking about our feelings."
Hospice, she says, is the perfect fit for her, and she finds it
more rewarding than oncology:

> One of our patients had lung cancer and was struggling
> to breathe, and we just sat with his wife for an hour.
> Just sitting. This would never happen in the hospital
> system—that's all just vitals, documenting, and com-
> puter work. The hospital setting thinks differently. It's
> all about the "pros" and about wellness. The mentality
> of, "We're gonna fix, fix, fix, fix." In hospice we get to
> ask the patient, "What do you want? It's your choice."

It's your choice, I think, because you're dying. There's
nothing to fix. But you didn't choose to die; when the lung
cancer metastasized, it chose for you. What if what you want
is to live?

I think about the day I spent with my own hospice patient,
Oliver—his heavy breathing and the flap of his upper lip as he
exhaled—and I wonder if there was a wreath at the hospice

in South Bend. I wonder if I could handle sitting in the Good Thoughts Room and staring at his name on a piece of paper. I wonder what it's like for the nurses to stare at the names of hundreds of their dead patients. I ask Pam what I'm most curious about, especially after her explanation of burnout among oncology nurses: how does she, or anyone, do this job for a long period of time? What does this kind of loss feel like, and what does this career involve, emotionally? And how honest was she being when she told me that she loves her job?

Pam starts her answer with a discussion of "perspective." She says that sometimes it's hard to focus on the job that needs to be done. "Your own life gets in the way," she says, "like with any job." A hospice nurse, while worried about her son's bad report card and the fight they had the previous night, still has to do her job. She walks up the stairs to a house in which a 35-year-old man, dying of brain cancer, refuses to eat the lunch his husband made. Pam talks about one of her experiences:

> As an administrator, I still take calls sometimes. Probably about seven years ago, I ended up taking call on a Saturday because the call nurse was sick, and I was really busy that day, and I hadn't been out in the field a lot. I was tired, and I wanted to get it over with. In this case, I went to a patient's home, a young breast cancer patient with three kids. I just remember the kids were

maybe like one, three, and four years old. It was clear to me that she wouldn't make it through the day. Her husband was there, and I looked over on the couch and saw those three babies in diapers and footsie pajamas, and I had to tell the dad that he was going to be a single dad that day. But I also had three other patients to get to. I was distracted, and I rushed through it with him. Eventually, I went back in and made sure he was O.K., and I sat with him for a while, but when I initially told him, I just wasn't present.

Maybe this is part of the difference between the loss that hospice nurses face in their careers and familial loss, or the kind of loss that leads to a permanent depression. "Your own life" can get in the way in their kind of loss. I wonder what it would mean for my own life to get in the way of Momma's death. "Hurry up and die, Momma," I'd think, looking at the time on my cell phone. "I've gotta run." Still, it's not quite the same thing.

Pam tells me that she loves her work. "It's great, the impact we have on families," she says. "Selfishly, going into homes and making such a difference makes me feel good. The families are like our patients, too. We affect lives. And again, it's all about perspective." Pam smiles at me, and then motions toward the window. "See? The sun is shining, it's a beautiful day, and I get to drive my car. I have the health to go outside and see these patients and make a difference."

I hate the word "perspective" and all the phony "glass half full"-like phrases that often accompany it. The word, essentially proposed as a solution to mental illness, was tossed around so much during group therapy. "It's all about perspective," the therapist, like Pam, would say. "It's about challenging yourself to not see 'gloom and doom' all the time." The therapist said "gloom and doom" so much that he eventually bought two plush dolls, designed by the brand Uglydoll, that he named Gloom and Doom. Gloom was a bat with five pointy teeth, and Doom didn't look like any animal in particular, but more like a turquoise potato with two yellow teeth. We were supposed to ignore Gloom and Doom, literally and figuratively. The therapist recited a research study revealing that the more a person smiles, the happier he becomes. "Fake it 'til you make it!" he exclaimed, following his refrain: "Power in perspective." Gloom and Doom were supposed to remain in the corner of the group therapy room, but they rarely did. Ivan liked to hide Gloom under his shirt, mostly because it made the uptight nurse visibly distraught. "For the love of God," she would say, frantically searching the group therapy room for Gloom, blind to the bulge of Ivan's shirt. "Will you people please stop messing with the therapy dolls?" Every once in a while, Ivan would hide Gloom and Doom in the bathroom or under our beds. "If you stand in front of the mirror and tell yourself you're attractive and you're worth it," the therapist would say, "you will start to believe it." I tried this once as I stood near the bathroom sink, and after a few seconds of repeating positive phrases to myself, I looked to my left and saw Doom sitting on top of the hand dryer.

"Thinking in a different way," or looking at something from a different perspective, is in part the premise of cognitive behavioral therapy, and I've tried practicing it countless times. But I haven't been able to shake the little nagging part of my brain that reminds me of the futility of the exercise. A debate takes place inside my head. One part of me says, "You're worth it," as the other says, "Don't believe it; you're a failure," and they go back and forth on different topics—my appearance and the size of my body, my career as a professor, my writing ability, my social life—until, eventually, the negative one is crowned the winner, that nagging queen. Father Dore preached perspective, too. Toward the end of our interview, he asked me, "What are some good things that came from your mother's death?" I couldn't think of any answer. Perspective has its limitations. Instead, I pictured a popular comic in which three drinking glasses are each partially filled with a yellow liquid. The first glass, smiling and raising his fist in the air, says through his thought bubble, "I'm half full"; the second, frowning, hands at his sides, says, "I'm half empty"; and the third, both hands raised and mouth agape, says, "I think this is piss."

After Pam talks about what "patient education" entails,

she uses the word "perspective" again. She mentions a cancer patient named Lucille, for whom Pam, when she was an oncology nurse at St. Anthony's, had cared. Later, when Lucille needed hospice care, she'd requested Pam's service. "I educated Lucille and her husband on the resuscitation process. She wanted to sign a Do Not Resuscitate, and I asked, 'Lucille, what does that look like to you?' Because it's not like it is on TV, where you do some coughing and it's painless, and then the family says a quick goodbye and then goes out to dinner or something." But Lucille still wanted to be "a full code," Pam shakes her head, "even though she was actively dying." On a Saturday afternoon, Pam walked into their bedroom and saw Lucille's husband trying to put the feeding tube in Lucille's mouth. "She was non-responsive, clearly, and he was standing over her, talking with her, saying, 'C'mon, sweetheart,' and just trying and trying with the tube," Pam says. "I tried to explain to him that she was non-responsive, but he just wasn't getting it. He had a different perspective." She continues, "He was just living in a different world. He kept asking me to help him with the tube. It was his own reality."

The way Pam says "making a difference" helps me understand how a career as a hospice nurse is humanly possible. The hospice nurses make a difference, which for them means that they helped a patient eat, or they talked to a patient and calmed him down, or they reassured the family that it wouldn't be tonight, that they still had a few more weeks with their loved one. But for the patients and their families, the presence of a hospice nurse portends death. This difference is crushing and permanent—there's nothing rewarding in watching a family member die. Even though I received education from one or two nurses about medication administration and application of gauze to Momma's wounds, I can't remember their faces very well, just the weight of their words. There might have even been someone who looked like Abby, but I wouldn't know. I could have talked to her for six hours a day for six months, and I still wouldn't remember. The nurses had transformed our home into a hospital, and inside it, Momma was dying.

Pam says she'd never experienced "true loss" until she was 60 (a year and a half prior to our interview) and she buried her mother-in-law. Then, a month before our interview, Pam's father-in-law died. When Pam went back to work a few weeks after the death of her mother-in-law, she ended up having to call a social worker to relieve her. "It was such a short time since she'd died," Pam says, "so it was too hard for me to be with the patient." Since her father-in-law's death, Pam has refused to see any patients, saying, "I haven't been by the bedside." She doesn't say when or if she'll return. She swamps herself in administrative duties instead. It seems that what Pam labels "true loss" has considerably affected her relationship to her job and her ability to perform, but this doesn't seem true for her "regular patient losses." Based on the stories

Pam tells me, I think it would be highly unusual for a hospice nurse to say, "Tomorrow is too soon for me to return to the bedside," if her patient had died the previous day.

What do you call a loss that's not true? "Career loss" is the only thing I can think of, but that just makes it sound like losing a patient is the same as missing a basket in the third quarter. I can't know what their type of loss is like—I just know, based on everything Pam said, that it's different. Maybe it is like losing a basketball game after you've put so much energy and time and passion into the season. But the nurses work from a set of assumptions, presupposing the deaths of their patients. Their kind of "loss" is anticipated, so even playing the game in the first place requires pretending. And they only get a glimpse of the patient's story—they see death, never life, or the patients' personalities and identities that are independent of their illnesses. When their patients die, they're able to walk out the door without the burden of clutching those dead bodies to their chests. And maybe my own loss is like holding a tube to a motionless mouth and saying, "C'mon, sweetheart," for a brief moment, every single day.

When Pam talks about the interview process for hospice nurses, her office phone beeps, and a muffled voice comes through the speaker: "Funeral Home, Line 1." "Did you hear that?" Pam asks. "We'll often hear, 'Coroner, Line 1,' too." She laughs, and then continues to talk about the expectations that newly hired hospice nurses have before they've "even gone out into the field." She says some candidates have great interviews, but they "bomb out in the field." Pam's job as an administrator often involves making sure that prospective nurses "can handle it." Maybe it's not a "true loss," but even so, the hospice nurse has to witness death on a consistent basis. Pam says that, on some days after work, she'll just drive around aimlessly in her car for an hour or so before going home. To a certain extent, it doesn't matter if it's a "true loss" for the nurses or not—rewarding work doesn't imply a lack of difficulty. Hospice nurses still need an escape at the end of the workday. Dealing with dying may demand some indulgence in fantasy. For Pam, this involves watching "mindless TV," like the *Bachelor* or *Dancing with the Stars*, and taking the long way home, turning up her car's stereo as she drives down the back roads.

"So when I hear someone say, 'I've always wanted to do this since I was little,'" Pam says, "I try to make sure that they truly understand what they're signing up for." If a prospective nurse says she's always dreamt of this career, Pam might ask her what those dreams consist of. "I'll ask the nurse, 'How does that look to you? When you're dreaming, what do you see?' Because they often have this beautiful notion, from movies or something, of being that sole comforting light for a dying patient, the patient's best friend. And that's usually not how it is."

When the prospective hospices nurses dream, do they dream of the moon? What happens when you've kept certain expectations with you for a while and, suddenly, you're faced with a reality that doesn't match? Is this where perspective comes in? Do you have to pretend that the reality is just as cool as your expectations, repeating, "This is amazing!" over and over while tri-cycling around cones until, somehow, you eventually believe it is?

After her discussion of the hiring process, Pam says, "As you are well aware, Rockford has all these rural areas and big farms. So we have lots of patients who were farmers." She tells the story of a glioblastoma patient who was a farmer, and when he got sick, his wife took care of both him and the farm. "They had this long driveway," Pam says, signaling length by stretching her arms out to her side, "and as I was driving up it, their horses would run alongside, and I would drive with the horses following me to these big barns in the back." She says that even before she opened her car door, she could smell fresh baked goods. The patient's wife was up before 4 a.m. to take care of her husband and the farm, and she was usually done with all of her work by the time Pam got to the house, around 11 a.m.

"The house was so clean, and there was always something in the oven," she says. Pam whispers the next part and beckons me closer. "There's *still* always something in the oven," she says, eyes wide, "because we found out that she keeps up the routine she had when she was taking care of her husband.

He's dead, but she still makes a plate for him and eats breakfast with him every morning."

I picture a small breakfast table, the farmer's wife sitting
across from her husband's ghost. Does she speak to him?
Does she throw out the breakfast he can't eat? I wonder if
she'll do this until she dies, too, scrambling eggs for his spirit.
What happens if you're living your own truth, in a world that
others don't inhabit? You're sure that the cardboard circle is
the actual moon, and you're sure that, after a difficult journey, you really did reach it, and you'll always remember it this
way? In that case, does reality ever interrupt your narrative
like a fuzzy "Funeral Home, Line 1," returning you to what's
"right"? I imagine that it might be comforting for the farmer's
wife to continue fixing his plate. And who are we to tell her
that she's not, "in reality," sharing a meal with him?

There was something surreal about being a patient in the
psychiatric center. I knew that "lights off" was at 11 p.m. and
"night checks" were ten minutes before that, at 10:50 p.m.,
and I knew that I took my pills in a plastic cup twice a day:
once in the morning, and once in the evening, administered
both times by a nurse. But sometimes I only figured out the
date based on the craft activity. I knew it was February 14th
when we wrote our names on paper hearts, and I had been
there for exactly two weeks. Still, there were several times
when I felt I wouldn't mind staying there longer than I was
required to. There are days, even now, when I think about

returning, not necessarily because I feel like I'm a danger to myself, but because it's comforting to be in a space almost removed from reality. It's a relief, I think, to relinquish control sometimes, like a character in a video game, letting someone else map out your activities and make decisions for you about things like when and what to eat, or what time to get ready for bed. When I think about returning to the psych facility, I feel a temporary peace. When I think about suicide, I feel something similar. Both present themselves as options for escaping the torment of everyday life, and all its routines and activities. I found myself wanting to be unaccounted for, a name on a heart that's visible only to the people in the group therapy room.

I might have stayed in the facility longer had I not been unexpectedly "brought back to reality." One night, a few minutes before "lights out," I walked into my room and saw something sticking out from underneath my bed. I bent down to look more closely: it was Gloom. I picked him up and squeezed his soft bat body. Then, I laughed—the hard and deep kind that's accompanied by a cough—and I continued laughing until the nurse said, "Quiet down now; lights out." I hadn't laughed at all during my time there, up until then, when I realized I wanted to leave.

There are a few times in my interview with Pam where I picture myself in Rockford, in the cul-de-sac of Abby's description, reading a book or eating dinner at the table in our open layout. Maybe we even had a farm. Maybe I'd been a popular senior at Rockford High, the type of girl who throws parties in the family barn when her parents are gone for the weekend. Fantasy frees, while illness controls. I wonder what it would feel like, or if it would even be fully possible, to get rid of the nagging queen forever. Still, I'd be bound by memory.

At the end of our interview, Pam says, "This is something I won't forget. To know that we impacted you, and you came back to talk with us—that's what we like to do. We like to make a difference." She smiles at me, and then holds out her hands for me to grab. I take them, and I smile back at her. "It's probably been healing for you, too," she says.

A few weeks after the interview, I send a "thank you" card that I address to "Pam, Abby, and all the Heartland nurses." The last line reads, "Thank you for everything you do, and everything you did for my family and me."

CHAPTER FIVE

The Estate Planner

Thursday was beef stroganoff and lemon pie. The woman who wanted to divorce her husband but feared to be alone loved beef stroganoff days. The mid-life crisis guy next to her didn't give a shit one way or the other; he wasn't hungry, but it was time for his smoke break so, "Goddamnit," he said, "where is that wet blanket when I need her?" He was talking about the nurse, our ticket out, the person who took the elevator with us down to the first floor and hovered over our fifteen-minute break, commenting on the passage of time and reminding us in her silent way that we weren't mentally stable enough to take in fresh air without supervision. "Ten minutes left," she said. "Tick, tick, tick. Finish your cigarette. Wrap it up."

For the patients in the psychiatric center, time was our ticket to normalcy. We spent our hours in the group therapy room mapping out our schedules for when we'd get out of there. 2 p.m. meant the lady with a bob and a bad attitude critiqued our future calendars. "Why do you have more than eight hours mapped out for sleep? Why aren't you allocating an hour for exercise? Why did you leave blank the hours between six and seven?" Busyness impedes self-reflection, or emotional thought; in order to be functional, we had to be mechanical.

Every day at 10 a.m. a therapist passed around a chart titled "When You Grow Up in a Dysfunctional Family." The chart mapped out labels: Lost Child, The Black Sheep, The Family Clown, The Hero—each one was supposed to correspond with the roles that patients played in their "dysfunctional" families. The therapist defined "dysfunction" as "a family's exposure to any kind of trauma"—things like conflict, neglect, abuse, loss, or addiction. The Hero is a perfectionist, over-controlled with a fear of failing. The Black Sheep is the family scapegoat, engages in impulsive behavior, never quite fits in, feels like a loser. The Clown hides pain with humor, is often scared, feels inadequate. The Lost Child is ignored, quiet, artistic, prefers solitude and has difficulty verbally expressing feelings. After I had been at the center for a week, the therapist gave me the Lost Child label. He said, in front of the group, that loss could cause certain people, like me, to remain stuck at the age they were when they experienced it. "To free yourself from being stuck," he advised me, "you have to fill the hours in your day with activities. You have to actively avoid thinking about the past by being consistently engaged with the 'real world.'"

Right after Momma died, I tried to lose my sense of the present in repetition. I listened to "World Spins Madly On" by The Weepies on loop. I reread the *Harry Potter* series— Momma used to read them out loud to my sisters and me before bedtime. I watched the same home video again and again—the one where I'm not yet a one-year-old and I'm screeching in my crib as my aunt Michele tries to dress me in my baptism gown, and Momma says, "She doesn't want to go to church!" I ate the same junk at the same time every day, wore the same dirty clothes, watched *Gilmore Girls* DVDs on loop while Sarah fell asleep in the bed next to me and the theme song, "Where You Lead" by Carole King, repeated throughout the night. I hid behind my blankets and wished for time to stand still.

After noticing that I'd been lying in bed all day for two weeks in a row, my dad tried to teach me the value of busyness, too. Shortly after the wake and the funeral, he had my sisters and me start our summer jobs at his printing company. Most of the tasks he assigned us involved "busy work"— hanging posters to add to the office décor, or organizing long cardboard tubes of old prints in the warehouse. After a few days of work, Sarah and I were climbing ladders and moving tubes around, and we started fighting. We screamed that the other was doing the job too slowly, or wrong, and we slung insults back and forth before we collapsed onto the floor and cried.

My sisters and I weren't successful at keeping busy, but it seemed to be my dad's method of survival. He buried himself in work. When he wasn't at the office, he was in the computer room in our basement, making business calls or sending emails. Once, on a night that I couldn't sleep, I went down to the basement at 3 a.m., and I watched him through the door—he was crying to Billy Joel's "Only the Good Die Young," and I saw his whole body shaking. Busyness wouldn't erase his feelings about losing his wife or cure his loneliness, but he still tried to distance himself from the past. In what spare time he had, he golfed or had dinner with friends, doing what he could to stay out of our house. A few months after Momma died, he decided that the house needed remodeling. I think that sleeping in the same room that Momma had died in was crushing him, and a remodel would take up more time and maybe even erase the marks that death had left. He needed something new, but I was still stuck resenting progress. Change scared me—we'd already had enough of it.

The remodel happened anyway—I had just started my sophomore year at Notre Dame, but I came home almost every weekend to spend time with Sarah, who was a junior in high school, and each time I came home, something was different. He expanded his and Momma's bedroom by removing the balcony and adding a bathroom with a rainfall shower and an office area; he repainted each room in the house; he removed the carpet from the living room and our bedrooms, and changed the basement carpet; he reupholstered the living room furniture, bought a new couch for his room, and he picked out new bed frames and mattresses.

I was angry with him for seemingly moving forward. The bathroom wall no longer had the faint Sharpie marks on it from Momma's physical therapy; my grade school desk— the desk behind which Momma would stand and look over my shoulder to correct the grammar in my stories—was removed from the upstairs office; the bunk beds that Sarah and I shared—we held hands through the space between the bed and the wall on nights when we were too anxious to sleep— had been replaced with twin beds; and he'd thrown out boxes of things, like our old report cards or childhood toys. I worried that with all the changes, I'd soon forget parts of my past and forget Momma. If I stayed "stuck," I could preserve my memories.

During the remodel, my dad spent even less time at the house. We didn't see him much, and when he was present, he usually just retired to his bedroom and closed the door. My sisters and I were always closer to Momma than to our dad— we turned to her for advice, and we'd choose to tell her, over him, the details of our lives. We wanted him to quickly fill Momma's role, but this was an impossible expectation—still, because Momma wasn't around and the house was quieter, his absence was even more noticeable. We weren't having many conversations with him, so if we wanted to get information about him or his whereabouts, we had to snoop. A few months after Momma died, we found an email on his computer that mentioned a dinner date with a woman named Mary Lee Turk, and it became clear that he was also "moving on" by starting new relationships. I was furious at him. It was so soon after Momma died that it felt like he was cheating on her, and although I didn't want him to be lonely, it felt insensitive of him to hide his dating life from us, and even to date in the first place. Instead of asking him about it, I stayed angry and passive-aggressive—on weekends when I was home from college, I'd smoke weed in the house or drink his alcohol from the cabinet, with the hope that he would recognize that I was struggling or in desperate need of help. He didn't notice, or if he did, he didn't say anything. And I felt a rage that came from not being able to slow anything down, and I wanted to scream all the time.

*   *   *

The night before my interview with Mary Lee Turk, I considered canceling it altogether. I stayed up the whole night, pacing and biting the skin on the inside of my cheek. I

worried, mostly, that the whole thing would be extremely uncomfortable. I'd recently seen a message appear on my dad's
phone that was from a different woman, so I assumed his relationship with Mary Lee was over, but I hadn't planned on
asking her anything about it. I planned, instead, to ask her
about her career as an estate-planning attorney—I was genuinely curious about how she perceived grief after witnessing
people planning for their deaths. I wondered what her clients
valued the most and what legacies they wanted to leave. Mary
Lee worked at the same firm as Momma, so I also hoped she
could provide me with a clearer idea of this time in Momma's
life. But more than that, I wished that facing her and finding out about her history and experiences might allow me,
somehow, to move forward. I don't want to be stuck in the
emotional age of a teenager, and I want to stop believing the
label the therapist gave me—Lost Child. I want to be able to
acknowledge my feelings, even the negative ones, and express
them—maybe this could improve my relationship with my
dad, and maybe it could stop me from feeling like my life is
on loop, like I'm calling out for Momma so much that I'm
shutting myself off from any kind of future.

The next morning, I arrive five minutes early at what I
think is Mary Lee's condo. But the gate is locked, and none
of the buzzers say "Turk." After standing in front of the building for a few minutes while people pass by me and give me

suspicious looks, I email Mary Lee, who tells me I have the wrong address—her building is the one next door, and when I walk up to it, the doorman immediately lets me in. Due to this miscommunication, Mary Lee and I are off to an uncomfortable start.

Her condo is pristine—her aesthetic is very different than my parents' or mine, and partly because it's so clean, it doesn't feel home-y, or lived in. I guess if you're in charge of keeping people's estates in order, it makes sense that yours should be exceptionally orderly. She's pristine, too. She has dyed blonde, almost platinum, hair, fixed in a bob; she's wearing a pearl necklace with matching earrings that make her J-Crew sweater look formal and elegant; she is freshly manicured; and she has a full face of makeup. In my white t-shirt, jeans, and dirty Converse sneakers, I feel underdressed, and even the two Klonopin tablets that I took earlier can't stop me from worrying that she must hate me already since I forgot to take my shoes off at the door.

I worry, too, that I will spill ink on her couch as I'm taking notes, or I'll fall into my anxious habit of crumpling paper into tiny balls and dropping them onto the floor. When I was in high school, Momma used to have me practice the art of eating lunch without picking apart a napkin. "You'll never get a job if the interview is at a restaurant or a coffee shop," she said, before scolding me for taking the tomato off of my sandwich. "You eat like a squirrel."

Mary Lee tells me that she's newly retired after a long, physically and mentally draining career, billing an average of 220 hours a month. A few minutes into our interview, I relax a bit, as Mary Lee seems easier to talk to than I'd expected. The part of me that's still 18 wishes she weren't—it'd be easier to make jokes about her later. I can tell that she's nervous, too, and it seems like she's trying hard to figure out how to relate to me. Avoiding eye contact and staring down instead at the coffee table, she looks guilty of something—maybe she agreed to do this interview to absolve some of it. Does she feel guilty about dating her dead friend/co-worker's husband? Maybe she's guilty about the time frame—she dated my dad very shortly after Momma died—and she's trying to give me her time now to make up for it.

Before I even ask her about Momma, she starts to talk about the first law firm where they met in the early '80s but specialized in different areas. "I remember your mom when I was working," she says. "She had a great sense of humor—she was wicked and sharp, and went in for the zinger." She adds, nervously, "But I don't have any really specific stories. I wish that I did." She looks down at her crossed hands and then says, "We were both so busy in our own areas, but I would talk to her at office parties, and that's where I met your dad, too. I just remember your mom being a lot of fun and very witty." I nod at this, but I wonder if she can sense my disappointment—in a way, I feel that getting specifics about this time in Momma's life could give me clues to my own life, or how to navigate it, especially as I'm around the same age now as she was when she worked there.

I pause before asking my next question, thinking Mary Lee might say more about meeting my dad, but she stares at me instead, and I'm eager to fill the uncomfortable silence. "I read somewhere that estate planning is the legal equivalent of heart surgery," I say. "Did you find it this demanding?" She has a long answer, and I can only pay attention to parts of it. Admittedly, when I hear words like "bifurcation" and "trustee," or phrases like "moving assets around" and "protecting clients from creditors," my brain automatically tunes out. I glance around her apartment for any sign of disorganization or clutter, but I focus back in on the conversation when she talks about asking clients questions about their inevitable deaths—one of the most difficult aspects of her job, she says.

Let's say I'm talking to a married couple, and I ask them something like, "What do you want to happen if you, the husband, pass away first, and your wife remarries?" The husband might respond, incredulously and with disgust, "My wife is going to remarry?!"

Or, I might ask them to think about what would happen if their children die before them, and people respond with things like, "Why would you say that about my child?" But it's something they have to think about. They just don't want to deal with it—they want it to all be behind the scenes. But we have to ask certain questions…we have all these different scenarios and "what-ifs." What if, for example, Caitlin is the only one who survives, but Sarah has a surviving spouse and kids? What would your dad want to see happen in that case?

We also always have to ask what our clients would want to happen if everybody in the family dies at once, even though the chances of that happening are very slim. And you always have to marry what that client wants with what will save the most money and taxes for them.

When she says the word "marry," I automatically think about her relationship to my dad, even though I'd rather not. It's strange to hear her use not just my name, but also Sarah's, in a hypothetical where I'm the lone survivor. Sarah has never met Mary Lee, and I'm certain she'd hate that Mary Lee brought up her name at all, let alone in a what-if scenario that demands her death. Mary Lee's interview was the last one I transcribed, mostly because I didn't want to think about my dad's dating history all over again, and I wasn't ready to hear her voice again right after our interview. I wanted time to process my feelings about their relationship.

I ask Mary Lee if she's ever dealt with a client who's had an extreme emotional response to her questions. She says, "Yes. See, we also deal with people after there's been a death. Like your dad after your mom died—that was really tough—but you try to be understanding and say, 'I'm so sorry for your loss.'"

The way she says "that was really tough"—her eyes wide and her voice heavy—makes me think that she's frequently heard my dad discuss his feelings about Momma's death. It's possible that Mary Lee is more aware of how he feels about it than I am. I realize, then, that this is one of the reasons I sought her out—my dad and I rarely have conversations like this, or open up to each other at all. We've spent so much time avoiding this kind of deeper communication, and I wish we could get those hours back. He prefers solving problems, mapping them out, rather than talking about them. Recently, on a family vacation in Hawaii, he had a long discussion with Meaghan and me about money for our future children's college education, the cost of housing in the future, and the importance of 401ks and investing in stock markets. The talk was confusing at first, especially since neither Meaghan nor I has expressed interest in having kids yet, but now, when I look back on it, I think it was his way of telling us that he was worried—that there was only one parent left and he was worried about his own health and our future security—and he wanted to "solve" this his way. He's practical, as well as generous, and he uses money as a way to solve, too. When Momma was first diagnosed with breast cancer in 2005, our next-door neighbors were moving out, and my dad ended up buying their house so that my grandma and my aunt could live there and be physically closer to us and to Momma. When my dad bought this house, he "solved" our need for additional help, but despite his best efforts, he couldn't solve Momma's cancer.

In 2010, my dad drove to South Bend after my roommate called to tell him about my overdose. He arrived a few hours after I'd been discharged from the hospital, and neither of us knew what to say. Money and planning couldn't solve my depression, but I could tell by looking into his eyes that he wished so badly that something could. He took me to a movie, perhaps with the idea that I could escape into it, and it prevented us from talking—when it was over, he gave me a long hug, and he asked me several times if I was okay, before he headed home. I was frustrated with myself for not asking him to stay, for not telling him that I was upset that I had failed in ending my life, and for not giving him a chance to know the messy parts of me. And a few months later, after I'd dropped out of Notre Dame and had returned to Oak Park to finish my degree at a school close to home, we kept trying, but failing, to connect. We cared about each other's lives but still didn't have many direct conversations, so my sisters and I snooped through his things—drawers, computers, file folders or notebooks—for information, and he snooped through ours. We all tiptoed around each other. Without Momma, we were all Lost Children.

I realize that, while lost in thought, I'd been staring at a wall in Mary Lee's condo, and I quickly look back toward her as she discusses her presence at her clients' funerals:

> I've gone to a lot of funerals, and it's tough. It feels odd for me to be there because, on the one hand, I care about the family, but on the other hand, I don't want them to think I'm just showing up to get the business. I was going to get paid after the fact, and probably paid a good amount of money, but I wouldn't want them to think that was the reason I was there. I just went because I thought it was the right thing to do.

I ask her how she builds a rapport with her clients. "They have to feel like you care," she says, "that I'm on their team." This reminds me of what Pam says to the hospice care families and patients, and I wonder if Mary Lee has an outlet or a space to vent that's similar to Heartland's "Good Thoughts Room."

She talks about clients who have very specific or strange requests. One woman, she says, wanted to be cryogenically preserved, so Mary Lee had to review the contracts with the preservation facility in Arizona, one of two in the country. "I think that's where Ted Williams' head is," she says, and for some reason, I'm surprised that she's openly talking about that. I guess I'd forgotten that her entire career centered on acknowledging death and its messiness, and I'd just assumed she wouldn't be interested in talking about body parts because she seems so "pure." I remember reading about Williams' head being stored in a steel can filled with liquid nitrogen. Mary Lee jokes, "I asked that particular client if she would even really want to come 'back from the dead.' I presented her with a what-if: 'What if you have great, great, great, great grandchildren—are they going to share their money with you?' I told her, 'I don't think so.'"

I smile as my mind jumps to an image of a lady, suddenly active after a century of being frozen and stored away, walking up to her great (times 10) grandchildren and telling them what year she was born as they stare back at her. I feel a little closer to Mary Lee after she shares more stories involving death's messiness. Maybe she won't be too mad when she realizes that I couldn't stop myself from performing my anxious habit: crumpling up pieces of my notebook paper and dropping them on her spotless white rug.

I ask her why she thinks that people care so much about "stuff," or why, after a death, it's common for families to fight over what's theirs. She answers:

When a parent dies, it brings up all the emotions from childhood—things like, "Mom always liked you best," or, "You always got your way." People focus on tangibles, like who gets dad's watches, and that's where feelings can get hurt, especially if there was a second marriage and the children of both marriages are fighting each other for family heirlooms. Maybe it's not even the thing itself, but what it represents. It becomes that person.

If you have something of theirs, then maybe you feel like you still have part of them. I think of Jim's watch in "The Gift of the Magi," his favorite thing, once his father's, and before that his grandfather's. A week after I left the psychiatric center, I bought a watch just to hear it tick. I measured time by its distance from Momma's death, the moments and events she missed—things like Sarah's prom, our graduations, our first jobs, our first career successes, our first heartbreaks and loves, new apartments, family vacations, holidays. I grew angrier with each tick.

One night, as I lay in my bed and listened to the ticking, I thought of the story of John B. McLemore, an antique clockmaker and restorer, who killed himself by drinking potassium cyanide, the substance that he used in his process of covering clock parts with gold. I thought about what it would be like to be able to swallow time, or to destroy yourself with the tools that you use to create beautiful things. I thought about how time seems to slow down when I smoke weed, and the calm that it brings me. I thought about what it means to have a terminal illness, and how much time any of us have. I thought about what Meaghan said once—that my sisters and I were projecting our anger over Momma's death on our dad—he was the one with all the time, and we wanted to steal more hours for her. I thought about how, when a tragedy occurs, people often think about where they were the moment it happened—how on September 11, 2001, some people were late to the airport and missed being on that flight. I thought about the time it took for my sleeping pills to kick in—the drowsiness, the dizziness, the beeping of the machine. I thought about how it wasn't Momma's things I wanted, it was Momma herself, and I thought about how the world moves forward even though it's dying, how chemicals invade coastal waters, and how some hospitals used to be gardens.

As Mary Lee continues to talk about the things that people covet after a death, I think of the things that will always remind me of Momma, some still at the house, some at my apartment and some at my sisters' places, and some long gone: her journals, her Contracts textbook, her gold stud earrings in the shape of an "X", the British Edition *Harry Potter* set, the Black Eyed Peas *Elephunk* album and Broadway Show Tunes CDs, Beanie Babies and American Girl dolls, the red pen she used to cross out the bad sentences in my school papers, microwaved eggs, Portillos hot dogs, TCBY parfaits, and Market Day hot lunches, the tan La-Z-Boy recliner, the *New York Times* crossword page, the picnic table costume that she made me for Halloween, the family of outdoor duck statues on our front lawn, *The Vicar of Dibley* box set, purple dog pajamas, polo shirts, and high-waisted jeans.

I think about the things that I associate with home. I think about how they didn't disappear from my memory just because the house looks different—they don't live inside the house. I remember Friday night board games when my sisters and I were in grade school—or one night, in particular, when Meaghan, determined to "beat the buzzer," accidentally whipped the plastic *Catch Phrase!* disc in my direction, and it ended up chipping my front tooth. I remember Momma propping me up on the kitchen counter as she taught me how to make scrambled eggs and told me not to be scared of fire; "snack parties" with my swimming teammates, for which Momma ordered Domino's pizzas and we all ate several slices before our practices; Meaghan and me dressing up as Ashlee Simpson and lip-synching her songs in my parents' old bedroom; my dad introducing me to the horror movie genre, particularly the *Hannibal* series, in our basement; my grandma's face as she accidentally ate a handful of dog treats that she'd taken from our kitchen counter—she'd thought Momma had said, "You can eat these," instead of, "You can feed her these"; Momma teaching me how to egg-beater kick to prepare me for water polo, grabbing my legs and rotating them as they dangled off the edge of her big bed; my sisters and me singing Billy Joel with my dad as he blared the CD from the downstairs speakers; the months after the remodel when Sarah and I fell asleep on our new mattresses to *Gilmore Girls* reruns, our version of "keeping busy." I've held on to these hours, the things that make me feel most alive.

*   *   *

Mary Lee starts to talk about what she can remember about sitting down with my dad and Momma to plan:

> Your mom wasn't terribly well at that point. I remember she had gauze on her arms and she was thin, but she was always thin in my memory. I remember her being in good spirits, and she wasn't talking as if she was going to be passing away soon. I knew she was sick, but at that point there was still some hope that she'd recover. It was sort of unspoken among us that more likely your mom would die before your dad, but I'm sure I didn't speak like that—I just wouldn't have. One of the things we do is health care powers and property powers of attorney, and we did them for your mom, and she named your dad to act as her agent to make medical decisions for her if she wasn't able to.
>
> My recollection of your mom was that she was like, "We've got business to do. Let's get this over with." Again, she was a lawyer. Your dad was focused on

getting it over with, too, although he was more ... you know [she laughs] ... *Ed*. He was lightening the mood as best he could, but still, it was the "let's get this done" mentality.

Momma's "let's get this over with" mentality echoes what Debbie Musso told me about their wig-shopping experience. As Momma's journal shows, she preferred speaking and acting on behalf of others, but while she was sick, she had to prepare, plan, and accept help from others. Together with my dad and Mary Lee, Momma had to speak on her own behalf about her own death.

When Mary Lee talks about my parents' responses when she sat down with them, I realize that my dad and Momma were probably much more alike than I had previously considered. On paper, the two of them always looked very different to me. Momma was a studier who excelled in school. She preferred English to math, and she was a quiet leader, shying from center stage. My dad did just well enough in school to pass, and he was very visible in his role as CEO of a company that had his name in its title. Although they had different ways of problem-solving, their values and priorities—the importance of things like family, generosity, faith, humor, and personal sacrifice—lined up, along with their worries.

Mary Lee returns to talking about discoveries about her clients. "A lot of stuff comes out of the woodwork when people die," she says. "I've found out, for instance, that someone's husband had a secret Swiss bank account. Once, a client had a secret love child." She continues, "We've had clients who make gifts to their mistresses, and they don't want to put that on their tax returns." And some people, she adds, want to have some sort of control over their families' futures, "trying to manipulate or change their children's behavior with a trust instrument." She says, "For example, the trustee won't give you any money if you have any felony convictions or if you have a drug arrest, and some parents arrange it so their children can't get access to any money unless they marry someone within the same faith—they're trying to protect their kids in their own way." This reminds me of my conversation with Debbie Musso, the idea of wanting to control something when you feel like you have little control over your own fate. People want to make sure the future goes the way they've imagined it, even if they're gone.

Mary Lee switches quickly between topics. She talks about how women in all areas of law face sexism, even if it's less blatant now. Her discussion of this feels familiar—I remember Momma making some of the same complaints. Mary Lee says she and Momma were often asked to get coffee by men in positions equal to theirs, and she says that many female litigators, feeling pressure to prove their equality, boasted about how much time they worked or how little time they spent with their families. She talks about her divorce and about caring for her mother, who suffered from dementia. She says,

"My mother didn't remember my name at the end," and she talks about her fear of dementia being genetic. Her mom died two years ago, when Mary Lee was 59. She mentions the things she inherited in her mother's death, and how some of those things are still stuffed in her closet because she hasn't "dealt with them yet." She says she doesn't "buy into the idea of an afterlife," and with a laugh, adds, "Nobody's ever come back to prove it to us." She reminisces about being an under-graduate and dreaming, then, of becoming a journalist.

She seems relaxed after an hour into the interview. "The real reason I went into estate planning is because it's about people and their stories," she says. "I couldn't care less wheth-er one corporation was merging with another—but I cared that we could do something that made it easier or better for people. And their stories are so fascinating." At this moment, she reminds me a bit of Debbie Musso—a doer—and like Momma's friend group, smart, hard-working, and headstrong. I can see why she and Momma might have been friends. I can also understand, even if only partially, why my dad might have liked her.

I feel comfortable with her, and I find myself confiding in her about some of the interviews that I've done. I tell her about the hospice nurse who thought she worked with Momma, and we laugh together. I tell her that I don't buy into the idea of an afterlife, either. I tell her about my job as a pro-fessor and my dream of writing multiple books. And I tell her about my dad, that my communication with him isn't always easy, that I used to wish he could be more like Momma, and that I wish I felt more comfortable opening up to him about my life—not just the successes, but also the struggles. She nods, and she looks at me in a way that makes me think she genuinely cares. She says, "It's true—the relationship is just not the same. It's different, but you know he loves you unconditionally." She talks a bit about the fears she had after her own mother died, and how she felt angry at her mother after she'd died for missing important events, like the birth of her granddaughter. "My mother was 86 when she died, but I was very close to her, and I'm still grieving. It's a loneliness and an emptiness," she says. "I don't know if that will go away. But we can just try living with it, missing them, and appreciating everything that they were."

I ask her what she's thinking about doing with all the spare time she has now. She says she's interested in interior design, and she might take a class or two to learn more about it. "Whatever I do," she says, "I'll want to feel busy. I like having my time mapped out."

*   *   *

In grade school, when I first began playing the trumpet, I had a trumpet teacher who gave me weekly lessons, but whenever he droned on about time signatures, I nodded off—I brought home the music that I was supposed to practice, and I asked Momma to hum me the melodies in the right tempo. She was the one who taught me about time in music, and I practiced my songs over and over again until I mastered them. I liked experimenting with the tempo, intentionally speeding up or slowing down, and I'd play some songs in the reverse, starting with the final note and going backward to the top. I loved that she let me play them as many times as I wanted for her—I could control when we'd stop.

Momma and I were in the old kitchen when she blared the song, "Dancing," from the *Hello, Dolly!* soundtrack. Carol Channing's voice pounded out of the boom box next to our oven. Momma held my waist and swept me across the kitchen floor as she loudly chimed in on the chorus: "And one, two, three, one, two, three—look! I'm dancing!" In that moment, Momma was Dolly, and I felt like Cornelius—"My heart is about to burst, my head is about to pop, and now that I'm dancing, who cares if I ever stop!"—and I wanted to stay safe in that song forever with her, our bare feet sliding in and out of rhythm on our cold kitchen floor.

CHAPTER SIX

The Embalmer

The summer after my freshman year of high school, Momma drove me four hours to Blue Lake Fine Arts, a music camp in Michigan where she'd enrolled me for a few weeks. Since I was too shy to introduce myself to my camp counselor and my cabin mates, Momma did it for me. "This is Caitlin. She's 15 and plays the trumpet, and this is her first time at summer camp," Momma said, as she helped me put lift my suitcase onto the top bunk. Outside the cabin, she and I hugged, and I whispered in her ear, "I'm scared. Don't go," right before I watched her get into the car and drive away.

All of the campers were supposed to audition for ensemble placements within the first hour after arrival. My cabin mates had all been at the camp in summers before, and they seemed like close friends. I trailed behind them and tried to understand their inside jokes as we passed hundreds of pine trees and walked for a long time, farther into the woods, where our auditions were being held. When we got there, a counselor told us to line up about 1,000 feet behind a small, wooden stage. We stood in line nervously, listening to the audition of each camper in line before us. One by one, campers stepped onto the stage and played their selected pieces, as three judges sat in chairs and faced them, listening and taking notes.

My legs shook as I walked up to the stage to take my turn. I'd prepared "The Little Fugue in G Minor" for trumpet, and as I put the cold, silver mouthpiece to my lips, I remembered what Momma said on the car ride as she massaged my neck with her right hand and steered with her left: "Just pretend I'm the only person listening."

I took a breath and began to play Bach's fugue the way I had practiced for Momma in our living room—loud and steady, with confidence. Since I'd memorized it, I closed my eyes so I wouldn't have to face the judges. With my eyes closed, I could hit the high notes. I played for just over three minutes, heard the judges thank me, and then stepped down from the stage. When I couldn't find my cabin mates, I began making my way back to the cabin by myself.

After just a few minutes of walking, I heard a familiar voice calling my name. I turned around to see Momma, who hugged me and then explained: "I was too curious to leave—I wanted to hear your audition, and I was standing behind a tree when you were on stage." I laughed and felt a huge relief—for a moment, it was just the two of us again. Then she faced me, and clutching my shoulders with both of her hands, said, "You were incredible. Your sound echoed through the woods, and it was even more beautiful than your practice rounds." She added, more quietly, "Much better than the other campers," and we laughed together, her arm around my shoulder, until we reached the cabin. "I'm really leaving this time," she said, as I watched her close the car door behind her. "I know you can do this."

On my last day of camp, each band held a concert for an audience of camper parents and friends. My woods audition allowed me a seat in the orchestra, the highest possible placement for campers. I was so relieved to see Momma in the audience that I smiled at her during my solo and accidentally blared the wrong note. But it didn't matter—right after the concert, she'd be taking me home, and when we'd get there, I'd be practicing songs for only her again, my comfortable audience of one.

For a year or so after Momma died, I imagined that she was just hiding—standing behind a tree, she was watching me, temporarily invisible but still, one day, capable of emerging.

*   *   *

I'm back at Drechsler Brown & Williams Funeral Home in Oak Park, Illinois, for the first time in almost 10 years. Though there are new flowers on the front yard, the building looks the same as it did on the day we saw Momma's embalmed body. It's a brown brick facade with white columns on either side of the front door. The Marion Street area of Oak Park hasn't changed much, either—it's a warm spring afternoon, and families sit outside Poor Phil's for seafood and Cajun cooking, the upper-class white women with chipped polish still walk into Salon 212 and Day Spa for a fresh mani-pedi, and tween girls with braces and scrunchies still buy heart studded friendship bracelets from Claire's Accessories. I'm following Charlie Williams' wife, Lynne, down the hallway to her husband's office, and it smells like mothballs and Monday Meatloaf at the psychiatric center, and my legs feel heavier with each step.

I have an aversion to endings. Once, in my early twenties, I had a panic attack at a movie theater because I'd remained seated when the credits stopped and the screen went black— since then, I've learned to exit before they stop rolling. When I was little and watching a musical with my family, I always cried right after the actors' final bow. There was something magical about witnessing a play—the sets shifted around so seamlessly, the accompanying music seemed to come from nowhere, and even if we were seated far away from the stage, the lights made it seem like the actors were always looking directly at me as they spoke or sang—but there was always that moment when the actors stop being their characters and even the play's biggest villain smiles broadly as he thanks the orchestra pit. What made my heart ache the most was exiting the theater and seeing the actors, wigs or costumes removed and makeup smeared, talking and laughing with their friends or family members. They had tricked me—I'd escaped into their fictional worlds but had suddenly been thrust out. When the audience's clapping grew louder as the main characters held hands and bowed, I wanted to yell at everyone to stop. "Life's not fair," Momma would say dismissively, when I complained that I couldn't stay in a fantasy forever.

Funerals and wakes are exercises in play-acting. There are directions for grief. We shake hands at wakes, we give flowers, and we sign the guest book. People deliver their lines—things like, "I'm deeply sorry," and vacant phrases masquerading as hope: "She's at peace now." "We will all be together again one day." There's a mourning soundtrack—sniffles when "Amazing Grace" is played on the piano and laughter as people share funny memories. There's an audience for death, but this audience generally prefers to see the "tidy" side—we're supposed to be comforted, not scared, by our own fates. Caskets are expensive, but they're pretty, and they contain. When funeral directors present the body with fresh makeup and styled hair, they shield the corpse's visitors from the messy part. It's easier for an audience to pretend that, after a certain period of time, grief goes away. People may stop listening after a while: they stop bringing food and care packages, they stop asking how you're doing, they stop looking at you tenderly, like you're going to break.

If, seven years after your mom dies, you send a drunken text to an old friend telling her that your depression has gotten really bad again, you might not get a text back. You have a certain amount of time after the coffin is lowered into the ground, and when that period is over, you crawl back into your own box and navigate the world without other people's sympathies or their scrutiny. These things are supposed to be wrapped up. I wonder if, in the mustard seed parable, villagers ever grew tired of hearing about Kisa's grief. When she knocked on families' doors, her child's rotting corpse clinging to her chest, did anyone tell her to "just get over it," or send her away?

A few months after Momma died, I watched a movie called *Two Weeks*, starring Sally Fields. Fields plays a mother, dying from cancer, who is trying to navigate her relationship with her children. She writes a book for each of her kids, a kind of instructional guide for their lives after her death, with little notes and anecdotes about mistakes to avoid and things/ideas/mottos that she found valuable throughout her life. This seemed completely unrealistic to me—in order to write this kind of book, Sally Fields' character must have, at least to some degree, accepted that she was going to leave her kids behind. Momma didn't want to die, and she was never going to be ready to acknowledge that she would, or even talk about the possibility. Although I understood this, I still felt paralyzed by confusion in the months after her death.

Momma controlled our house, and then her illness controlled it. She directed, and she mapped out our schedules. After she died, it was my dad's turn. An hour after her death, he sat my sisters and me down on the couch in the basement and told us what we could expect to happen in the next few days. He gave specific information about Momma's wake and funeral, telling us the times for each one and the number of people we'd be expected to talk to. He talked for about 20 minutes, and after that, it was kind of like we were dismissed. It was all very final. Part of the reason why I remember his talk after Momma died is because of its brevity—as soon as he finished talking, the basement felt empty, and I could feel instruction's absence.

When a play ends, the audience gets up and follows signs for the exit. For a few hours after Momma died, I lay in my bed and thought I might not ever be able to get up again—without her and her direction, I worried that I'd forget the basic rules of existing.

Now, as I shake Charlie's hand, I become aware that I'm doing the opposite of "wrapping things up"—I'm re-opening. I didn't have to interview Charlie, but I did it anyway—maybe, by talking to him, I'm intentionally playing Momma's wake on loop. Maybe it's a kind of self-sabotage, and I don't believe I deserve to move forward with my life when Momma's life stopped before it should have, so perhaps I'm intentionally holding myself back at the age I was when she died. But I think, too, that I'm scared to stop grieving, even if I could—if I stop, if I lay her body in the forest like Kisa does with her son, then maybe I'll forget even more of her. What would it mean for my grief to be "contained"? Death is an ending, but it's the ultimate escape, and I fantasize about it because it brings me closer to Momma, and most days, I don't want the fantasy to stop.

I smile broadly at Charlie, a "play" smile like Momma taught me, as we sit facing each other in the office of the home.

Charlie, 56, with white hair and a red face, is a third-generation embalmer and funeral director. He's wearing an Irish knit sweater over a collared shirt, and unlike what I'd expected, he seems jolly, like he'd be a good person to get a beer with. "I pride myself on avoiding stereotypes," Charlie says while grinning. "I use the term undertaker, and it's an archaic term, but for me it's a sense of pride." He clarifies that an undertaker is someone who undertakes whatever is necessary to do the job, and in his case, do it well. "Because a funeral home is like a farm without animals," he explains. "We have a physical plant, and we're constantly preparing for what's going to happen, like farmers—they fertilize, sow, reap, care for animals, paint their barn, maintain their equipment—and that's what we do here."

He graduated from Worsham College of Mortuary Science in Wheeling, Illinois—what he calls the "Harvard of embalming school"—in 1983, but he says he's always been in the business. He's lived above four funeral homes in his lifetime—all in Oak Park. In his days, a kid could do a lot without having a mortuary license. Even though he was only 16 when he was picking up bodies in hospitals, he always believed his childhood was normal.

"Don't be afraid of the dead," he warns me, with a finger wag. "It's the living that will get you." He folds his hands and leans forward, his stomach pressed against his desk, and he looks me up and down, like he's deciding whether or not he should hire me to work for him.

He breaks his stare to say that he remembers Momma, and he brings her up as he walks me through the embalming process, using her as an example. "We get her body in the prep room—and then we elevate the head, position the hands and arms together, and then set the features—which means closing the mouth and eyes and initially creating a pleasant expression." He continues: he disinfects her eyes, mouth, nose, and any "unpleasant areas." The typical injection point is in the clavicle area, and when he explains this, he uses his own head to represent Momma's, and with his left hand, he pretends to inject fluid into his clavicle. "And you remember," he says, "we start with a picture of her when she was alive, so we try our best to cosmetically recreate that likeness."

Even though I can acknowledge that it's strange, and even morbid, for Charlie to use Momma as an example, I'm still able to listen to him without feeling queasy. It almost feels like picking a scab—it hurts as you're doing it, but something compels you to continue, anyway, until you can see new blood. I continue smiling and nodding at Charlie as he talks about the presentation of Momma's body.

The length of the embalming depends on the kind of death, he says, explaining, "If you get somebody who had cancer or a debilitating disease that caused them to waste away, they're gonna need more work." Charlie injects an embalming fluid (a mixture of formaldehyde gas and solution with dye and humectants) into her arteries, forcing the blood to flow to the fingertips and feet to create "rosy toes, pinky soles"—a mortuary school expression telling the embalmer he got good blood distribution. He aspirates the body, puncturing the intestines, lungs, liver, spleen, gallbladder, stomach, and heart to suck out any liquids—excess embalming fluids, urine, and waste. He washes the body with antiseptic soap, cleaning the fingernails and trimming the nails, and cleaning the eyes and ears. Then there's the application of cosmetics themselves. He applies a translucent cream to the body to retard dehydration, and then he clothes the body and places it in the casket. Finally, after checking the body the next morning, Charlie says, "Things are in order," to himself—his ritual.

"I say this after every embalming procedure and even sometimes before I go to sleep," he whispers to me. And some nights, before bed, he plays Bram Stoker's "Dracula" on his flat screen. He's seen it ten times. "For 400 years, Dracula had a different woman every night. He never ages!" Charlie explains, beaming at me from across his desk.

Embalming is not just a business for Charlie; it's an art form—the dead body, his canvas. An embalmer's goal is restoration, his end result—a done-up body—can be retouched and ultimately presented to the world, to the deceased's loved ones as they remembered him/her. The deceased is dressed in an outfit chosen by the family, including underwear, and the viewing of the restoration commences the loved ones' grieving processes. Restoration is a physical covering of scars, in a way distorting the reality of the body's battle with life. Charlie disposed of Momma's wound V.A.C., and with it, the infectious materials that it managed to suck out, and then covered up the evidence on her body. Once we prayed above her restored body, we put dirt over the box, emptied it into the ground, and said amen.

One of the greatest compliments Charlie's ever gotten, he says, was from a woman who had just buried her mother: "Mom looks great. She should have come here sooner."

I think of Momma's body in its casket—the overapplied blue eye shadow that she never would have worn, the stiffness of her hands, folded together. As my sisters and I knelt before her body and pretended to pray, Meaghan blurted out, "What the fuck? This looks nothing like her." Her body was on center stage, and Meaghan was right—I remember thinking that Momma looked like a sculpture at a wax museum, her cheeks painted red to present the illusion of life, and all of the wake guests were there to pose with her likeness.

When I stood next to the casket as visitors lined up to view her and say their goodbyes, I remembered a time when I was little and my family was snorkeling near the shore in South Carolina. My mask was too tight, and I tried to tell Momma through my mouthpiece, but what came out was just a gurgle. I choked on the water that seeped through the snorkel's top. My heart was racing, I couldn't breathe, I screamed silently inside my mask. Momma swam to me, removed my mouthpiece, loosened the latches on my goggles, moved her own mouthpiece to the side and then said, "You don't have to do this if you're scared." But I looked around and my sisters were doing it, and my dad, effortlessly, and I wanted to see what was underneath me, too. I put my mouthpiece back in and watched the coral in one spot as I hovered in place. It wasn't the kind I'd seen in science books, the pretty kind. It looked like brains, dozens of them—dead, colorless brains getting picked apart by tiny fish.

Charlie leans back in his chair, crosses his arms over his stomach, and begins to tell me about the time when he wished he could have taken "the Crisco out of someone's husband in order to fit him in the casket the family wanted." After he says this, he stretches his arms to the side and winks at me as he adds, "I'm talking huge, here." That day, Charlie searched online for a larger casket, costing $200 more than the original, and paid for the difference himself. "I up-served them," he beams. "But I didn't tell the family, because how much is your reputation worth? Like, gee, Mr. Smith, your brother is obese, so we're gonna go with the jumbo model, which will cost you more money." He would never "toot my own horn" or ask the family if they like the way the body looks, but he says the transformation is his favorite part of the job. "You're taking this terrible—let me rephrase—this deceased person who looks like shit," he says, while grinning, "and you're making a difference—bathing, grooming, adjusting, preserving, and presenting." The worst thing that could happen in his business, he explains, is if someone said, "I was in your place yesterday, and what did you do to Mr. Anderson? He looks like hell."

Charlie shifts gears and runs his fingers through the casket catalog that sits next to his desk phone. "This particular casket is a good investment," says Charlie, who stops his finger on the image of the Kentucky Rose, "because we all wanna go out big." The Kentucky Rose features a Premium Delicate Pink Crepe Interior, an Embroidered Pillow, and an Adjustable Bed and Mattress. The Orchid Finish with Lilac Shading runs along its sides. Its ad instructs consumers to

"Think Pink." It can hold an overall weight of 240 pounds, and included in the price—$1,299.99—is a limited warranty against manufacturing defects.

My eyes widen as I learn the price of a "good investment," and Charlie, perhaps, sees my shock. "Listen, don't criticize people because they do this," he says, "because when it comes to the gloom and doom of selling caskets—there's always going to be a dead body." He continues, "Americans can afford to grieve. We can afford posh delivery units, Cadillacs to go to the grocery store, brown eggs, and range-free chickens, so if people have a certain way that they want to honor the death of a loved one, they're the ones who want it."

"When people come to me," Charlie adds, "I stress why I serve them. It's because I want more. I want to be the concierge of the funeral business."

I picture Momma's body on the preparation table, Charlie's service. He jots down a few details before beginning his work: White. Female. 52 years old. Breast cancer—double mastectomy, no reconstruction. The photo my dad gave him shows Momma holding a puppy by its belly and pressing its face against her right cheek. She's in the backyard of our house and wearing a bright blue shirt that matches her eyes and blue jeans. Her hair is short, straight, and blonde. She's smiling—genuinely, not posed—at the puppy. She's healthy—it's a pre-cancer photo—and she's tall and lanky, maybe 140 pounds. I imagine Charlie setting the photo down and then looking down at her body, naked on the prep table. There was no fat on her body when she died.

As Charlie pushes the casket catalog to the corner of his desk, my mind escapes to a moment in 2012, when I was 23 and living in my dad's house in Oak Park. I had a therapist, then, who recommended that I try something called flotation therapy—floating might allow me to experience some relief from my anxiety and depression, the therapist said, adding that I could sign up for an hour-long session at the Chicago Stress Relief Center. He explained the scientific benefits to sensory deprivation, including increases in dopamine and endorphin levels. A flotation tank contains about ten inches of body-temperature water, and in the water, there are over 1,000 pounds of Epsom salts that allow a person to float effortlessly. Each tank is insulated against sound, and the float typically happens in total darkness. Before I stepped into the tank, a technician gave me instructions: "Put in the provided earplugs, enter the tank backward, close the hatch lid, and then relax on your back." After closing the lid, I extended my arms, hitting them against the sides of the enclosure. I was alone with my thoughts. The tank was about the same height and width of Momma's coffin. I thought of her embalmed body, arms at her side and eyes closed.

I tried the technician's suggested position—"head back, arms crossed over your chest, legs separated an inch or two, like you're relaxing in bed." Because it was my first time floating, the technician recommended that I turn on the blue underwater light so that I would at least be able to see my surroundings while getting used to the sensation. I was naked, as he'd suggested, and I stared down at my pale stomach, wondering how, during the hour-long float, I'd be able to focus on anything other than the things I considered "odd" about my body—my breasts, my stretch marks, my big toe, the mole underneath my right eye. Epsom salts sting sensitive skin, and I became aware of my paper cuts, my hangnail, my leg shaving accident. The salt caked in my ear, and I took long, deep breaths through my mouth to calm myself down, but the lid to the tank seemed like it was caving in on me, and my stomach felt like it was expanding, like it would swell to the size of the tank, and I'd be stuck, and they'd have to cut open the tank to pull me out, and everyone would stare at my nude body as it was on the brink of exploding. My head felt too heavy for my neck. I remembered reading that a cockroach can live for weeks without its head, its body responding to stimuli without awareness, until it dies from dehydration.

I listened to the sound of my heartbeat, and I closed my eyes. I saw Momma in scrubs, the nurse pressing the cold stethoscope to her chest and then lowering it to listen to her lungs. I crossed my hands over my heart, and I thought of Momma calming me down after an asthma attack: "It's okay, sweetie. You're safe now. You're alive." I ran my fingers through the water and then through my wet hair, which was already straw-like from all the salt, and I thought of wigs and wounds and the moment before Momma's body was wheeled out of the bedroom, and I wished I could live for weeks without a head. I thought of my sisters and me trailing behind Momma's coffin to the altar, our legs heavier with each step— wasn't the tank supposed to make me feel lighter? I wanted to get out of the tank, to breathe outside air, to shout at the tank technician that I was still there, that he shouldn't forget about me, but I was sure that if I screamed, no one would hear me, so I kept my eyes closed and put my arms down to the side, aware of my impending burial. I waited for what felt like days for the music to play over the room speaker, the signal that the session was over. My hands were shaking when I got out of the tank, and they stayed that way for almost an hour afterward, and as I stared down at them, I wondered if I was just one of those people for whom the world is not made, and if I just didn't belong here or anywhere.

*   *   *

After a little more than an hour into our interview, I'm getting used to the home's musky scent. It smells familiar, like the wet towels that I would leave on the floor that would cause Momma to yell at me about the mess. I suspect that it's so familiar to Charlie that he's become inured to it. I get the sense that he feels similarly about the naked bodies he's accustomed to seeing on the prep table—it's not strange nor overwhelming to stand over a cold, naked, lifeless body; it's his job, and he's seen this for almost 40 years. Is he desensitized to death? I ask him if his business ever takes its toll on him. How does he cope? He pauses for a few seconds, and then sighs. It's the first time during our interview that he's not smiling.

He explains that while he's embalming, he separates the physical body from the deceased person's story and background. "I learn about the person eventually, of course," he says, "but only after I'm done embalming." The only thing he looks at before embalming is the picture of the deceased person, and only that way can he become an artist, reconstructing original masterpieces. He began the method of dissociating the body from the background at age 16, the year when, with the help of his father, he embalmed his mother's body. Except to him, it wasn't his mother, but just another canvas. "When we closed my mom's casket," he said, staring out the window, "I bawled like a baby. And then, all of a sudden, I stopped. I know she's dead, O.K.? But she was groomed, washed, laid out, and respectful." He pauses, and then adds, "That's all I'd like to say about it."

"You know," he says, looking away from the window and back at me, "Oak Park is relatively small, and we're so blessed to have recurring business, but sometimes, when people see me at Jewel-Osco or Poor Phil's or somewhere, they'll

get angry and say things like, 'I am so sick of seeing you.'"
That bothers him, he says, because he strongly believes in the
service he provides grieving families. "I can't change what
happened to you," he says, "but I can make part of it meaning-
ful and comforting. I'm not the creator of this havoc." Early
on in his career, he would write down a list of things to say to
the families as he showed them their loved ones in the caskets. On the top of his list, he wrote, "Things are in order."
"The emotional side is this: there's your loved one, and the
last time you saw them they were in that damned hospital bed
with all these tubes and all these machines and all this crap
around them. And now, when the family sees them, their eyes
closed, for the last time, all you want to do is say, 'Things are
in order.'"

He turns back toward the window.

"How old were you when your mother died?"

"Eighteen," I respond.

"Hmm." A pause, and then he says, "I was mature as a
16-year old—picking up dead bodies—no 16-year-old was
doing that—but in other ways I was so lacking…"

I nod.

"My mother—ace-in-the-hole," he says.

"What do you mean?" I ask.

"I mean, I knew all things were possible, because she was
there."

I imagine Charlie at age 16, looking down at his mother

on the preparation table. I imagine the raising of the right jugular vein, the trimming of the nasal hairs and eyebrows, the shaving of the legs with the mini trimmer to avoid razor burn, covering bruising on one hand by placing the other over it—a "trick of the trade." Perhaps, for his mother, he chose the Monticello Casket in Solid Cherry Wood: light and strong, a reddish-brown color that would darken with age. *Things are in order.*

I had a dream about you, Momma. Your head, floating—heavy blush and blue eye shadow—above my outstretched hand.

*   *   *

I was in charge of the music selections for Momma's funeral. The Communion song was "You are Mine"—its chorus swells with the line, "Do not be afraid, I am with you."

After Communion, I stood behind the organ, gearing to play "Amazing Grace" on my trumpet. I hid behind the music stand and pointed my bell toward the ground. The notes during the first verse reflected my shakiness—weak and tentative.

But I knew I owed it to her. When the second verse came, I raised my bell high above the pews and let her direct me, recognizing through music her presence. I blew into the horn as loudly as possible, with a blare that enveloped the hollow church, a fortissimo that functioned as a final *fuck you* to the illness that prematurely robbed her of her life.

How sweet the sound.

CHAPTER SEVEN

The Lost Child

Momma got her own room in the hospital—something she liked to brag about. When I walked in, she was listening to the playlist that I made for her on her iPod.

"The Black Eyed Peas," she said, while bobbing her head. "They're bouncy."

Her room was a mess, but that's how she liked it. On the windowsill next to her bed was an empty Kleenex box, a few books, a Portillos fast food bag, "Get Well" cards, a hairbrush, a makeup bag, and hand sanitizer. I moved a bag and a flower arrangement off of the chair next to her bed, and we sat in silence for a few moments.

"Come on," she said, "I want to show you something."

She started to get up, and then she motioned for me to help lift her.

"I thought you weren't supposed to—"

"Shh," she interrupted. "Let's break some rules."

I held her arm as we walked slowly down the halls of the hospital, trying not to get spotted by her nurses. When we got to her destination, the Maternity Ward, she pointed beyond the glass. "Look how cute all the babies are!"

We watched them for a while in their individual habitats and tiny white hats, cradled by blankets and sleeping soundly.

I laid my head on Momma's shoulder and whispered, "I love you."

*   *   *

In the Buddhist parable of the mustard seed, Kisa gets a happy ending. She realizes that what's "true" is impermanence—the parable leads the reader to believe that this epiphany gives her peace. Her journey seems short. She's able to accept her own loss after hearing about other people's losses. She goes to the Buddha for a miracle—to cure her dead child—and although the Buddha cannot bring her son back, he brings Kisa back to herself. She understands and accepts herself after collecting, a sort of miracle of insight. She's freed.

It's the neat version, the fable. I wanted my own search to bring me peace, to solve my problems, and to cure me somehow. I wanted my journey to do something powerful, to mirror the resolutions in the stories that Momma used to read to me—I hoped for an ending like Harry Potter's, all evil defeated, or I hoped that it would yield some great treasure, a magi's gift. I hoped that each interview would help me to feel more whole, and I hoped that each interviewee would serve as a version of the Buddha, offering me instruction, guidance, support, purpose, and maybe even a miracle. I knew that there wasn't a mustard seed that could reverse time or bring Momma back to life, but I hoped, still, that collecting could bring me comfort, and I hoped that by talking with and hugging the people who saw her last, I could feel her somehow.

Like all things, the interviews had to come to an end. I got to a certain point in the interview process when all of the stories started to sound the same. Father Dore is grieving his parents, especially his mom, and he can't listen to "Be Not Afraid" because of this grief. Debbie Musso discussed how she has pictures around her house of her dad, and she can't help but notice how much her son looks like him. Pam and the hospice nurses took care of dozens of Denise Garveys, patients with terminal illnesses who, like Father Dore's mom, had fear in their eyes before they died. Mary Lee Turk still hasn't unpacked the things she inherited from her mom's death. Charlie Williams grieves for the mother he lost at sixteen years old. In my research, I also reached out to Dr. Kathy Albain, Momma's oncologist at The Cardinal Bernardin

Center at Loyola Hospital in Maywood, Illinois. Dr. Albain didn't have time to sit down for an interview because she was in another state having to take care of her dying mother.

The interview process, as a whole, was messy. It was grueling and painful at times. The interviews left me with more questions than I started with, and I felt confused and lost, similar to how I felt right after Momma died. There were many times when I felt that revisiting these people and places was making things worse for my mental health. I reverted back to behaviors and patterns that I used to cope when I was 18. After each interview, I smoked weed and cried myself to sleep. I binge-ate ice cream in my bed, and for weeks, I didn't leave my apartment at all. I canceled a few classes that I'd been scheduled to teach, and I stayed under my covers instead. I lost focus and drive, so much so that my therapist prescribed me Adderall. The Adderall made me feel normal, if only temporarily, and I felt so irritable and useless without it that I began taking more than I was prescribed. If the interviews weren't the cure, then I had to find something. I experimented with different doses of my anti-depressants and anti-anxiety medications, and I stayed up at night, waiting to receive some sort of sign that I would get better from a God that I didn't believe in. I frequently thought about how I was letting Momma down, and I got angry with myself and with those around me. I lashed out at my girlfriend, and I avoided my friends and sometimes even my family. I felt desperate and lonely and insecure.

I can't easily summarize what I've collected, or my feelings about the process. I longed for things that I didn't, or couldn't, get from the interviews. At some points in my conversations, I felt like the Buddha, trying to offer comfort as best I could, even though I had hoped for the reverse. I wanted Father Dore to heal me through certainty—not necessarily the certainty of God's existence, but the certainty of *something*, something that matters and is worth believing in. He felt the most real to me when he said that he sometimes asks himself, "Is this shit real?" but I still wanted him to know for sure. I wanted the hospice nurse to have actually lived in that moment with me. No one's perspective felt sufficient enough—the moments of Momma that they shared with me didn't feel big enough, either, and I felt frustrated. I felt like I had failed. When they shared their experiences of loss with me, I discovered, like Kisa, that what's "true" is impermanence, but it doesn't make it easier that we all suffer, does it?

"This Thanksgiving," Momma writes in the same journal where she discusses her fears about her leukemia treatment, "I am grateful for clutter. It is in clutter that I see my children's passions. It is in clutter that I feel the warmth of my family. It is in clutter that I discover clear thought. It is in clutter that I find a clear path."

The stories that I've collected are cluttered. They're the piecework that everyone has to do in order to live. Through collecting, I learned that none of us really has the answers—we pretend to have answers, and we pretend to have control, and we come up with our own ways of getting through our lives and finding clear paths, but they are contradictory and incomplete. We distract ourselves or re-direct when things become too overwhelming, or there are too many things we don't know. We watch each other. We use other people as markers to see if we're doing things right. Because what we do know is actually scary: we're all going to die. It doesn't matter when we die, or how we die, although some moments and some methods are less harsh than others—it just happens, and we watch ourselves get old and our bodies change, and our desires evolve, and we experience good kinds and bad kinds of growth, and this is kind of a slow violence, but we all suffer it. We are all Lost Children, to an extent.

Still, I made discoveries after rifling through the clutter. I was always shy, and the interviews got me to talk. They got me to tell my story through writing. I'm now a little more fearless after the process of collecting and writing. I'm a little more familiar to myself. I felt more familiar to the people I interviewed, empathizing with their suffering and feeling their warmth. And, perhaps even more importantly, collecting has reminded me that I have not forgotten. I began this process by wondering what it would mean for me to lay Momma to rest. But I did the opposite of laying her to rest—I brought her stories back to life, making her more real to me and less of a stranger. I worked to remember her. I was carrying around her dead body with me before, and now I carry the parts that are alive.

*   *   *

My dad once told me how he hurt his finger, how he remembers the buzzing, siren-like sounds of the lawnmower and the crunching of the bone. He was three years old and watching his own dad mowing back and forth, finding comfort in the even clippings and in the constant hum. He wanted to help, so as his dad talked to their neighbor, he leaped off the porch and tried to sweep away some of the leaves that had gotten caught underneath the mower. But as he reached under, the blade made a quick cut across his finger, severing the top so all that was left was a nub and bone. He was rushed to the emergency room with his mother, while his father stayed behind to try to find the top of his finger in the grass. He never found it. His finger will always be missing its nail.

When Momma died, I felt a similar sensation, like something had been cut from me, something that I couldn't get back or find even if I looked for it. I searched anyway.

Momma's writing shows that she always kept searching, too. Her journal entries reveal her desire to fully understand herself, and she analyzes the path her life took, as well as the idea that her disease could negatively affect her feelings about herself and her relationships with family and friends. Although she expressed her insecurities, it seems that she was working on overcoming them. In doing so, she found out what mattered to her, the meaning that exists in small moments and stories. In one journal entry, she finds hope in the *Harry Potter* books:

I read a few chapters of *Harry Potter and the Prisoner of Azkaban* to the kids tonight. The author, J.K. Rowling, describes the use of a patronus to protect against dementors. Dementors are evil black-hooded beings that suck the happiness out of those who are near them. The defense against dementors is to create a patronus, or shield, by summoning to mind a time during which you were happy. Albeit fiction, the device of a patronus is an effective way to face difficult issues, situations, and decisions. I try now to remember happy events or moments when I feel sucked into a depression. I try to savor life's small joys.

There were times during my interview process that I returned to the feeling of my childhood when I believed stories made everything possible. Momma introduced me to the magic of stories. And she taught me how to write. I told her story the way she taught me. I continued writing even when I doubted myself. In collecting pieces of her story, I started to trust my own voice.

The day after Debbie shaved Momma's head, Momma and I sat in her bedroom and watched reruns of Planet Earth together. Our favorite scene was "Invisible Worlds." Plankton, tiny creatures virtually invisible to our eye, are an entire universe of life forms. The camera zoomed in on the microscopic phytoplankton, which provide 50 percent of the oxygen we breathe. Certain varieties have complex diamond patterns, snowflakes of the sea. All life on the planet depends on them.

My whole world depended on Momma's. But I'm trying to embrace the present, and I've learned to admire smallness. Some days, I go on car rides with my sisters, and we listen to bouncy music and sing along, off-key, and we laugh as we recall stories from childhood, and I feel free.

On February 24, 1998, Momma wrote in her journal:

The weather was beautiful today. I enjoyed listening to the girls' laughter as they played this morning.

I went off to find a science book for Meaghan and found Beanie Babies instead. Sarah and I lunched at Nordstrom's, and then we went to TCBY. I polished off

Caitlin's Chocolate Chip Cookie Dough Shiver—too fattening, but oh so good.

Caitlin did her multiplication flashcards with no fuss. I learned of an interesting potential cure for leukemia, which is undergoing human trials at Northwestern Hospital. Genetically altered lymphocytes are introduced into the patient's blood. Results so far are encouraging.

We watched *Hercules* tonight with the kids. The world seems brighter.

Throughout the process of collecting, I kept breathing, beating, existing. I went to therapy. I learned to embrace my own contradictions. I wanted to die, but I wanted to get better. I listened to my heartbeat. I thought of Momma. And now, some days, when I get out of bed, I start with small movements—I touch my head and my shoulders and stretch down to my toes, to remind myself that they're still there, to ground myself, to remind myself that I am still alive.

ACKNOWLEDGMENTS

Grateful acknowledgment is made to the editors of the publications in which excerpts from these chapters first appeared: *Post Road Magazine, The Baltimore Review, JuxtaProse Magazine, Little Fiction: Big Truths, Foliate Oak Magazine, Apeiron Review*, and *Matter Press*.

I would like to thank the Northwestern University MFA program for the support, encouragement, and feedback that I received throughout the path to my MFA. I am especially grateful to my advisors and manuscript readers, S.L. Wisenberg and Rachel Jamison Webster, who challenged and inspired me, and helped me develop creatively, intellectually, and emotionally.

It is with enormous gratitude that I acknowledge the people who allowed me to interview them, without whom this manuscript would not be possible: Debbie Musso, Father Thomas Dore, Pamela Weiss and the nurses at Heartland Hospice, Mary Lee Turk, and Charlie Williams. Thank you so much for sharing your stories, as well as my mother's stories, with me. I am so grateful that you allowed me into your homes and into your lives, and each one of you is an inspiration to me.

I am so grateful to my family—Sarah, Meaghan, my dad, and Dorothy Hogan—who gave me permission to tell their stories and gave me the support I needed to earn my degree. I love you even more than you know.

I am grateful to all of the friends, extended family, and peers who supported me through the writing process, and especially those who took the time to read early drafts: Melanie Greenspan, Molly Tyler, Molly Sprayregen, Ryan Kavanagh, and Katie Zanazzi.

Thank you to everyone at Homebound Publications—especially L.M. Browning—for believing in my manuscript and reminding me that my voice is important.

I want to thank my partner's parents, Hilarie and David Terebessy, for their support and their generous supply of baked goods, which helped me through long nights of writing.

Last, I want to thank my partner, Nina, for her love, patience, feedback, advice, and care. I would not have been able to take on this project without you, and I am so lucky to have you in my life.

ABOUT THE AUTHOR

Caitlin Garvey is a Chicago-based writer and English professor. She has an MFA from Northwestern University and an MA in English Literature from DePaul University. Her nonfiction has been nominated for multiple awards, including *The Pushcart Prize* and *Best of the Net*, and has appeared in *The Baltimore Review*, *Post Road Magazine*, *The Tishman Review*, *Little Fiction: Big Truths*, *Matter Press*, *Ragazine*, *JuxtaProse*, and elsewhere.

Visit her at caitlinhogangarvey.com